The Trailside
Cookbook

The Trailside Cookbook

A HANDBOOK FOR HUNGRY CAMPERS AND HIKERS

DON AND PAM PHILPOTT

FIREFLY BOOKS

A FIREFLY BOOK

Published by Firefly Books Ltd. 2005

Conceived and produced by

Elwin Street Limited
79 St John Street
London EC1M 4NR
www.elwinstreet.com

First printing

Publisher Cataloging-in-Publication
Data (U.S.)
Philpott, Don.
   The trailside cookbook: a handbook for
hungry campers and hikers/ Don and
Pam Philpott. — 1st ed.
[144] p. : photos (chiefly col.) ;
cm. Includes index.

Summary: Guide to cooking
and eating outdoors,
including information on
nutrition, food planning,
setting up camp, cooking
methods, equipment and
recipes.

ISBN 1-55297-952-0
(pbk)
1. Outdoor cookery. I.
Philpott, Pam. II. Title.
641.5/ 78 22
TX823.P555 2005

Library and Archives
Canada Cataloguing in Publication
Philpott, Don.
   The trailside cookbook: a Handbook for Hungry
Campers and Hikers/ Don and Pam Philpott.
Includes index.
ISBN 1-55297-952-0
   1. Outdoor cookery. I. Philpott, Pam II. Title.
TX823.P42 2005   641.5'78 C2004-904040-5

Published in Canada by
Firefly Books Ltd.
66 Leek Crescent
Richmond Hill, Ontario L4B 1H1

Published in the United States by
Firefly Books (U.S.) Inc.
P.O. Box 1338, Ellicott Station
Buffalo, New York 14205

Designer: Tracy Timson

Editor: Diana Steedman

Printed in Singapore.

Contents

INTRODUCTION

Every year, the pace of life gets faster, road traffic gets more congested and the pressures of urban living grow more intense. It isn't surprising, therefore, that more and more people escape to the great outdoors to get away from the crowds and the daily rush in search of fresh air and exercise and their own peace and quiet. From Alaska to Atlanta, and Aberdeen to Auckland, there are millions of people who can't wait to head out into the countryside every chance they can find.

Fortunately there are still huge tracts of country and wilderness to explore, from meadows and mountains to canyons and coastlines. There are tens of thousands of miles of long distance trails and bridle paths and cycle tracks. There is also a constantly changing environment as every season provides new panoramas and challenges. You can get so much more satisfaction from your trips if you are able to identify the birds, trees and flowers that you see along the way. You will appreciate it even more if you can recognize animal tracks and different geological and geographical formations.

In North America walkers cover more than 20 billion miles a year. The National Parks in the U.S. attract 277 million visitors annually with 1.9 million people hiking into wilderness areas to camp, while Australia and New Zealand offer almost unlimited opportunities for outdoor enthusiasts. Canada's national and provincial parks attract almost 25 million visitors a year for walking, hiking and camping. In Great Britain more than six million people regularly walk in their national parks and countryside.

However, you don't have to heave on a heavy pack and hike for days to enjoy the great outdoors, although this is certainly the best way to explore the real back-country. Just spending a few hours away from urban living and the television can be enough to recharge your batteries. Exercise is another wonderful benefit, although the majority of people who venture into the great outdoors claim to do so because they love it and not purely because of a desire to get fit. There are also many other pluses and food is one of them. The finest restaurant in the world cannot give you a view as stunning as that from the top of a mountain that you have just climbed. No diner can produce a meal as satisfying as the fish you have just caught and cooked, and who knows why, but coffee always tastes so much better when you sip it by the campfire under the stars.

Very few outdoor enthusiasts go walking or cycling just for the meal at the end of their day's exertions, but a good meal can really cap off a great day. Over the last few years, there have been enormous strides in the development of camping equipment and especially in lightweight stoves and accessories. Cooking on the trail is actually a pleasure and an opportunity to enjoy some great cuisine with good friends in wonderful surroundings. The aim of this book is to encourage you to be adventurous in your approach to trailside cooking. You don't have to rely on a can of beans for every meal or eat only dehydrated foods.

For many years, we were members of a backpackers' club that held an annual competition to see who could produce the finest gourmet meal on a single gas camping stove. The meal had to consist of four courses. Two prizes were awarded — one for the best campsite menu and one for the best meal cooked at the highest altitude. It was amazing how adventurous and how creative people were when cooking at 10,000 feet (3,048 m) and higher.

While most of us will not have to go to such heights to follow that example, there is absolutely no reason why your results should not be just as mouthwatering. With the right ingredients you can eat in style and as you recognize more wild plants, you will be able to add fresh herbs, leaves, fungi and other edibles to enhance your dishes. With a little planning and the right cooking equipment, you can create meals that are exciting and delicious as well as healthy and nutritious.

Enjoy!

CHAPTER ONE

WAY TO GO

Most people visiting the countryside still prefer to walk. They may drive to a trail head or a parking spot but they then get out and walk. If they are out for just a few hours, they carry a day-pack with wet-weather gear and a few essentials, including some food. If they are hiking into the backcountry they use a large pack to carry everything they need for the duration of their trip. This is where skill is needed in selecting the right gear because you don't want to have to carry more weight than is absolutely necessary. Modern equipment, including stoves and cooking utensils, is light and it is not necessary to compromise on quality.

If you are cycling off road, you can carry a little more gear in panniers but again weight is a critical consideration. However, if you are one of the growing army of off-roaders with a 4x4 vehicle, weight is not a problem and you can pack a full-size camping grill if you want to. Even if you are only out for a day there is no reason why you shouldn't park somewhere that has a fabulous view, get out the grill and cook up a feast before heading back.

In some parts of northern Europe and in many places in North America, pony trekking is very popular. Riders can roam the open countryside while most of their gear is carried by pack horses. It is surprising how much equipment you can carry in this way so when you stop to make camp, you should have everything you need to prepare a great meal.

LEAVE ONLY FOOTPRINTS

National parks and remaining wilderness areas are a universal asset to be protected for future generations. Everyone therefore who enjoys the outdoors must be a conservationist, enjoying it to the full and minimizing impact. In recent years, millions of acres of forest and natural country have been devastated, homes destroyed and lives lost because of wild fires. Most authorities issue regulations and warnings about fire hazards. Never light fires where the danger levels are high.

There is always a responsibility to others to be prepared. If you are heading into back-country or plan to be away for a few days make sure you have the right gear and adequate supplies, that you know how to use a map and compass, first aid, how to light the stove, and have checked the weather forecast. Above all, make sure someone knows about your plans and when you are due back.

- If you take it in, you must take it out. Leave no trace of your visit behind and if you spot someone else's litter, cart that out as well.
- Light fires responsibly and don't let them get out of control.
- Don't trespass, don't dig up plants or collect rocks or historical artifacts.
- Leave gates or openings just as you find them — open or closed.
- Don't pollute water supplies — bury human waste in the ground and make sure it is at least 100 feet (30 m) from water courses.
- Observe all warnings and regulations posted by the authorities.
- Respect the peace, solitude and tranquility by keeping noise to a minimum.

IN AN EMERGENCY

S Stop and take stock.
T Think each step through before acting.
O Observe your supplies, surroundings and capabilities.
P Prioritize what's to be done and then follow the plan.

A WORD ON WEATHER FORECASTING

Never head into the countryside without first checking the forecast and while you are away always keep an eye on what the weather is doing. By constantly monitoring your surroundings, you will usually have enough warning to put warm or wet-weather gear on, and start looking for somewhere safe to ride out a storm. Knowing how to collect water and light a fire in any conditions could determine not only your enjoyment of the adventure, but whether you survive or not. Always carry an emergency kit in a waterproof pouch or tin.

If the temperature suddenly drops it could signal the approach of a cold front and that also could mean rain. Learn to recognize cloud formations:

- **Cirrus clouds** are always very high and in wispy streaks. They usually mean good weather but if they build up in cold climates, coupled with an increase in the wind, a blizzard is likely on its way.
- **Cumulus clouds** are lower, white and fluffy and a sign of good weather. However, if they start to pile up on each other, there may be a storm coming.
- **Stratus clouds** are low and gray and generally mean rain, while small, wispy scud clouds blown before the wind normally presage bad weather.

Another way of forecasting is to observe nature's own weather forecasters. If there is heavy dew when you wake, the day will probably stay dry. If there is no dew, it will probably rain. Cattle sense approaching rain and will herd together and face away from the direction the rain is coming. Spiders can sense rain and don't spin their webs if it is going to be wet. If it is going to be windy, they will busily spin extra strands to anchor the web, and if it is going to be fine, you will notice spiders' webs everywhere. Many flowers close their petals long before the first drops of rainfall and some trees turn their leaves. The undersides of the leaves appear much lighter, almost silvery, and this is a sure sign of approaching rain.

If you are in a remote area, it is especially important to be aware of the weather. In the hills, storms often blow up quickly and conditions can deteriorate rapidly. Look out for deer because if a severe storm is coming they break cover and make for lower ground. So, if you observe changes in the weather that could affect your safety, it is a good idea to follow the example of the deer and head down into a valley and be safe.

NUTRITION

If a normal adult male stayed in bed all day he would need about 1,000 calories just to keep his body functioning, his heart beating regularly, and his temperature up, without losing weight. If an adult female hikes out in the cold, she would need to increase her calorie intake both for energy and to keep warm. If she happened to be backpacking in the hills and carrying a heavy load, her calorie intake needs to soar to 3,000 to 4,000 calories a day or more. A man would need an even higher calorie intake.

The Sierra Club has calculated that you need two and a half times as many calories to gain 1,000 feet (305 m) of elevation as you do to walk at sea level for one hour at 2 mph (3.2 kph). For example, an adult, depending on weight, needs between 350 and 500 calories an hour to cover 2 miles over rough but relatively flat terrain. To cover the same distance in the same time but ascending to 3,000 feet (915 m) that same adult would need between 850 and 1,250 calories.

The following statistics show the number of calories burned through exercise for adults weighing 130, 155 and 190 pounds (60, 70 and 85 kg):

Activity (1 hour)	130 lb/60 kg	155 lb/70 kg	190 lb/85 kg
Backpacking	413	493	604
Cycling (10 mph/16 kph)	236	281	345
Cycling (off road)	502	598	733
Hiking cross country	354	422	518
Horseback riding	236	281	345
Walking (uphill)	354	422	518

Knowing what to take with you and why is critical when heading off on the trail. Work out what activity and energy requirements your trip will involve to determine the level of calorie intake you will need. If the calories you consume equal calories you burn, you will have enough energy from your food for your trip. You might even put on a little weight as the exercise and activity converts body fat to muscle, which is heavier.

If your calorie intake is too low, you will burn body fat and lose weight. This is an inefficient way of providing energy as it takes about 10 percent more oxygen to release energy from body fat than from carbohydrate, which means there will be less oxygen available to pump through the muscles and you will tire sooner.

Even if you are out walking for just a few hours during the cold months, you will need more energy just to keep warm. In hot weather, your energy requirements may be lower but your liquid requirements increase. Sweating can lead to dehydration and hypothermia in the cold, and dehydration and heatstroke in hot weather. It has been estimated that a walker carrying a 35-pound (16-kg) pack in difficult terrain in very hot weather can lose up to 1 3/4 pints (800 ml) an hour from perspiration, and this is in addition to normal daily water loss of about 2 3/4 pints (1.3 l) through breathing, sweating and urinating.

It is vital to drink lots of liquids. Water is the most essential nutrient of all, as it is great for getting fluid back into the system, but it doesn't replace essential minerals and electrolytes lost through sustained sweating. You can replenish these by drinking diluted sports-type drinks and plenty of liquids in the forms of soups, stews and tea.

When you are on the trail you can push up your intake of carbohydrate and fat because these are readily converted to glycogen, the fuel needed to drive muscles and keep energy levels high. You can also snack to keep the fuel tank topped up so that you don't deplete carbohydrate stored as glycogen in your muscles and liver.

If you choose a high-fat diet you will get more calories from less food and this will reduce your pack weight: 1 tsp (5 ml) of butter (fat) contains 45 calories, more than twice as many as is contained in one teaspoon of sugar (carbohydrate). Protein is calorie-rich but energy is wasted converting it into glycogen. Fat tastes good so we get the pleasure of eating it, and it slows down digestion so there is a more even absorption of body fuel, which makes us feel full. Fats take longer to digest and convert into fuel but they provide a more sustained energy level. However, fat is only metabolized if the body has enough carbohydrates to get the reaction going.

If you need a quick energy fix consume simple carbohydrates. You can sometimes feel the surge of energy as the sugars get into your system. The downside is that after the initial high, your energy levels can drop significantly. For maximum energy on the trail, therefore, consume fat together with complex carbohydrates and protein.

FOOD PLANNING

Careful planning will ensure that you not only have enough food but that it is the right food. You will need to know how many people will be traveling with you, how long you will be away, what terrain you will be covering and what weather you are likely to encounter. Once you know that, you can plan the menus, and amend or adjust to take into account likely weather changes and cooking conditions.

Another consideration is climate. Fresh produce will perish sooner in very hot weather and you will need to drink a lot more water. Meals take longer to prepare in extreme cold or at altitude, so if you are on the trail during very cold weather carry more fuel and plan a high-fat, high-carb diet. Pack foods with a low water content (i.e., crackers instead of bread) as they are less likely to freeze. Setting up camp in extreme wet involves keeping your gear as dry as possible before you can concentrate on cooking. This is when a great meal cooked under tough conditions will boost morale and take minds off the weather. If it's all too much, then the snacks and comfort foods really come into their own.

FOOD CHOICES

Fresh foods always taste best but there is a limit to how much you can take if you are planning to be away for several days. We once went on a canoeing trip in Ontario's Algonquin Provincial Park and ate fresh meat for a week. Even though it was June, the water was so cold we suspended our meat supplies in waterproof bags under the canoe. The older the meat became the longer we cooked it just to be on the safe side, but we are both still around to tell the tale!

Many breads, biscuits and crackers can be safely kept for several days. Hard cheeses last a long time, as do rice and pasta. Peanut butter lasts well and is best repacked to reduce bulk and weight. Take measured portions of powdered mixes in plastic bags ready for making trailside biscuits and pancakes. Clarified butter is a better choice than margarine, and carob rather than chocolate, for hot climates, as these have higher melting points.

Dehydrated foods are light and quick to prepare. Manufactured dehydrated meals are nutritionally balanced and readily available — and generally delicious. Simply add water, bring to a boil, simmer for a few minutes and eat. We always pack some manufactured dehydrated meals because apart from providing "fast" food when you are really tired or

up against the elements, they also make excellent emergency rations. Most dehydrated meals have a long shelf life so that if you don't use them on one trip, they can be reserved ready for the next.

While there is a place for these products in emergencies, that is not what this book is about. Dehydrated foods that you have prepared yourself can be included in your menu planning. Drying is an ancient form of preserving food by removing the moisture on which bacteria, molds and yeasts can grow. You can dry fruits, vegetables and meats to reduce bulk, make them lighter to carry and extend their shelf life. Thinly sliced deli meats such as turkey, chicken, beef and ham all dehydrate well and make excellent snacks that do not need reconstituting, or they are ideal to take with you to add to soups, stews and other recipes. It is best to freeze home-produced dehydrated foods if they are not going to be used for some time, but they can be safely stored in airtight bags in a cool place for a few days before you head out.

Do-it-yourself dehydrating is easy when using either a conventional oven or a commercial dehydrator. A commercial dehydrator usually has several trays with automatic heat and air-flow controls. Unless you plan to do lots of dehydrating, save the expense and use your kitchen oven.

- **Cut large items** like apples, peaches, apricots, pears, peppers, zucchini and onions into thick slices. Smaller fruit and vegetables can be dried whole.

- **Take a large baking tray** for each shelf in your oven. One tray will hold up to 2 pounds (1 kg) of prepared produce evenly spread out. Make sure there is enough room for air to circulate freely around the food.

- **Preheat the oven to 150°F (65°C).** Place the produce on the trays into the oven. This initial heat drives the moisture from the food. When the surface of the food feels dry, reduce the heat to 140°F (60°C). This is the most critical phase because you don't want to dry too fast or the food will taste leathery. This final drying phase can take between five and eight hours. The oven door should be slightly open so that the moisture can escape and if the oven doesn't have a fan, use an electric fan in front of the open oven door to ensure good air circulation.

- **Every 30 minutes or so**, rotate the trays and turn the food occasionally to ensure it dries evenly and does not stick.

- **To dehydrate an entire meal**, for example, a stew or similar, simply spread the meal evenly on a tray and dry in the oven in the same way.

- **Once dried and cool**, the food can be stored in sealable plastic bags and kept in a cool, dark place indefinitely.

✺ **This symbol on recipes and listings indicates when ingredients can be dehydrated.**

When you use the dehydrated produce in a recipe, simply add water and allow time for it to reconstitute. A good rule of thumb is 1 1/2 cups (350 ml) water to 1 cup (250 ml) dried produce. Don't add too much water or the produce will go mushy. If it does need more water, you can add it judiciously during the soaking process. Soak overnight. Alternatively mix with water in a tightly sealed plastic bag after lunch and allow it to reconstitute as you walk during the afternoon so that it is ready to eat for dinner. Most produce needs two to three hours to reconstitute. If you are in a hurry you can pour boiling water over dried fruit and vegetables, let stand for a few minutes and then drain. Dried vegetables being added to soups and stews do not need soaking and can be added directly to the dish, which must then be brought to a boil and simmered.

Herbs and spices take up so little room that you should always carry a selection to add flavor to meals. Many herbs have other benefits as well. Basil, for instance, helps suppress nausea and vomiting; ginger is excellent for settling upset stomachs.

Comfort foods are an essential part of your trail larder. Few things are as comforting as a chocolate bar when you are wet and feeling weary. Always have a selection to eat as a treat when you are feeling down, or as a reward when you have successfully accomplished a tough part of the route.

Energy drinks are generally 6–10 percent carbohydrate — great for both energy and to support your immune system. However, sports drinks are best consumed before and immediately after exercise and water should be drunk during exercising. This is because sports drinks require more digestion, while water is absorbed faster.

Food safety is important especially in hot weather. Even in the backcountry you should practice good hygiene — wash your hands and keep your utensils and pots clean using biodegradable soap. Disposable wipes are useful for quick cleansing. Double-wrap food and don't allow contact that can lead to cross contamination. Keep food in airtight containers and don't open packets until you need them.

Trailside tips:

- You can easily make your own sports drink. Simply combine 1 cup (250 ml) natural fruit juice with 1 cup (250 ml) water, add a pinch of salt and shake well.
- Hard cheeses last well on the trail, especially those that have a wax coat. Extend the life of cheddar or other hard cheeses by coating them in paraffin. It's simple: melt the paraffin in a pan and then, with a pastry brush, apply a coat to the outer rind of the cheese. Ensure there are no bubbles in the coating. Allow to dry, then repeat until there is a solid smooth coat.
- No recipe is sacred and you can always add dried, rehydrated vegetables and meats. Add special treats such as sun-dried tomatoes or dried shitake mushrooms.
- Raisins can be added to a wide range of dishes for sweetness and extra calories.

Nature's larder Depending on the time of year and any regulations regarding harvesting of plants and animals, you may be able to supplement your diet with berries, fruits and nuts and many edible fungi. If you are close to water or the coast, there could be fish, shellfish and edible seaweeds. One of the pleasures of being in the wild is being able to recognize which plants and fungi are safe to eat and which should be left well alone. Many plants have medicinal or therapeutic properties that can be useful along the trail. Willow bark can be chewed to reduce inflammation and pain; the juice from aloe can be used to treat sunburn and bites — snap open a spiky leaf and rub the juice on the affected areas; lemon grass rubbed on your skin will keep mosquitoes away. You won't find all plants in all habitats and regions, so it does pay to identify those that you may come across. (For recommended identification guides, see page 142.)

CHAPTER TWO

TRAILSIDE KITCHEN

When selecting your overnight or base camp, choose your site carefully so that you will be comfortable and enjoy a good night's sleep.

First off, make sure that you are not trespassing. Then check out the area for signs of animal tracks or droppings. Different regions of the world have varying levels of hazard from wild animals, so take precautions where necessary against critters raiding the camp overnight for food. Set up the kitchen well away from the sleeping tents. Try to avoid positions under dead trees or very tall ones, which are more likely to get struck by lightning, and never camp in a dry gulch, at the bottom of a valley or next to a stream. It is not only colder here, you may get washed out if it rains heavily. Conversely, don't camp on top of a rise because you will be too exposed.

The best place to pitch your tent is an area just beneath the brow of a hill on the leeward side. Find a spot with low, natural cover so that if it does rain, it will not become too muddy. Ideally, it should be almost flat, with a slight slope for drainage, and sheltered from the prevailing wind. If you do have to camp on a slope, always sleep with your head uphill.

Clear the area of sticks and stones and anything else that might damage your tent and jab you as you try to sleep. With luck you will find the perfect spot that will be exposed to the rising sun in the morning, to dry out your tent and warm you up as you rise and prepare for the day, and tuck into a hearty breakfast.

SETTING UP CAMP

Unless the weather is bad, it is a good idea to set up your kitchen and cooking area some distance from the sleeping tents. Select a site that is flat and near some trees that will offer some shade, although setting up the kitchen under overhanging branches could mean you have to deal with drips and falling debris should there be a downpour.

SHADE AND PROTECTION

Shade offers protection from the elements for both your cooking area and your tents and in the camp kitchen, protects food from the sun and the fire from the wind. If you cannot find natural shade, create your own by building a screen using branches, a tarpaulin or a groundsheet. If there is heavy snow, pile it up to create a windshield. In very hot or wet weather, make a roof over the cooking area for protection from the rain. A makeshift roof should be high enough to allow you to stand up straight and move around beneath it, and allow smoke to escape.

LIGHTING

A good flashlight or headlamp is absolutely essential and each member of the party should have one plus a spare set of batteries in a waterproof container. A headlamp is invaluable. It is great for cooking, walking around the campsite at night and reading in bed. Many headlamps have multiple functions, allowing you to concentrate the beam or in an emergency to activate a pulsating strobe to signal your position.

Camping lanterns powered by kerosene or liquid petroleum provide good campsite lighting. However, they are bulky and you do have to carry the fuel. Battery lanterns are safe to use inside the tent. Candle lanterns can be used inside a tent for reading before you turn in for the night, but always use them with caution — a candle can melt tent fabric in the blink of an eye — and extinguish them before you doze off.

STORAGE

Keep the entire camp area clean and always ensure you clear away any dropped food in the camp kitchen area to avoid attracting animals and insects. It is a good rule never to store food in or near your tent. Keep all food (and other items like toothpaste and deodorants) in storage containers. When not needed, hang food from a tree branch well off the ground and away from the trunk if possible. Some North American trails have bear-proof lockers specifically for storing food in the backcountry. If there are no trees or lockers, dangle your food containers over an overhang or pile up all your equipment around the food and place rocks, pots and pans on top. If an animal interferes with the pile the falling pots might just frighten it away. Food can be sealed in plastic bags inside a closed knapsack so that the scent does not attract animals in the area or pesky pests. Keep dried foods in waterproof containers — you don't want them getting wet accidentally or prematurely — and stand the containers on rocks and cover with a tarpaulin for added protection.

Keep perishable foods in a cooler, if you take one, or if you are near cold, fast-running water, you can use this as a natural cooler for a day or two. Place the food inside a watertight bag. Attach one end of a length of rope securely to the bag and submerge it. Secure the other end of the rope to a tree trunk or around a large rock. If the water is not too deep you can push some sticks into the river or lake bed around the bag so that if the rope comes undone, the bag will not wash away. In very high temperatures, ensure you check carefully that food has not gone off.

Take as much trouble to gather up your trash. Store it in large, tightly sealed plastic bags that will trap any smell and that can be compressed for carting out.

COOKING METHODS

Nothing beats cooking a meal over an open fire. The food seems to taste better, you can utilize the embers (not the flames) to bake potatoes and root vegetables, and you can sit around it and enjoy the conviviality of each other's company. However, in many of the world's wild regions it is prohibited to light campfires, and many areas will post fire hazard ratings on approach highways or in the offices of parks.

Nonetheless, where it is safe and legal there are two options for an open fire: a teepee-type fire where pots are suspended over the heat, or a "T" fire, where the fire is lit in the top cross part of the T and its embers are raked into the bottom part, and used for cooking. The hottest embers are in one half of the cooking area and the less hot embers in the other half, giving one area in which to cook fast, and another in which to simmer or keep food warm in its pan.

Damper or stone fires are best built in a pit. Wood is used for fuel and two or three large, flat stones are positioned in the center of the fire to become hot. It is absolutely essential the stones be of non-porous rock, otherwise they may shatter when hot and send fragments in all directions. Once the fire is burning well it can be collapsed so that it rings the stones, and the pots are then placed on the hot stones for cooking. One or two large stones can be positioned on the perimeter of the fire where they will not be so hot, and be used to keep cooked food warm. The stones can also provide the base for a grill for even more stability for pots or a Dutch oven, or for use as a griddle.

BACKPACKER STOVES

When using a camping stove, create a flat base on which to stand it, and position it to benefit from the windshield to ensure the stove stays alight and the flames are able to heat the pot. Keep spare fuel away from the lit stove.

If it is raining or snowing hard when you erect the tent, pitch it so that the opening is protected as much as possible from the elements. Pack up stones or logs in a semi-circular wall to create a windbreak. Use your knapsack to create additional protection against wind and rain. You can then sit in the tent and cook in the opening, ensuring that there is a lot of ventilation. Have a container of water close by, in case the stove flares up or the pot spills and burns you. By the time you have finished eating your meal you will not only feel so much better, the weather may have improved.

Stoves are more convenient to cook with than open fires: they can be set up in most situations, be instantly aflame, the temperature is controllable and they have minimal impact on the environment. Their downside is that the fuel they require must be carried.

Small stoves are safest when placed on a firm, even surface such as a large flat rock. As a general rule never cook on a stove inside a tent because of the danger of a flare-up or build-up of carbon monoxide. In extreme conditions, it may be necessary to cook in the entrance of a tent but only if there is adequate ventilation.

There are many types of stove available from the lightweight, compact single burners to double burners and large family camping models that need to be carried by vehicle.

A number of different fuels are used. Gasoline (petrol) and kerosene stoves use liquid fuel which vaporizes on its way to the burner. Here, it combines with oxygen in the air and is ignited. The fuel is contained in a cylinder or flask that connects to the stove via flexible tube. The fuel is commonly available, but it does smell and can contaminate food if it leaks. These stoves tend to perform better than other types in extremely cold weather or at high altitude.

Liquid petroleum (LP) stoves run on propane, butane, or a mixture of the two and are by far the most popular worldwide. They are lightweight, convenient and effective. You can buy pressurized canisters of different capacities depending on the length of your trip or the number you are cooking for. Full canisters are not heavy but all have to be carried in (and out). A single burner stove screws into the canister and a valve turns the gas on and off, and some models have automatic ignition. The flame can be regulated, and therefore the temperature, by how far the valve is open. If it is windy, the flames are blown laterally and therefore much of the heat is wasted. At altitude, it takes much longer to heat anything because of the difference in pressure, and for this reason LP stoves are less effective than liquid fuel (gasoline or kerosene) stoves in very cold weather.

The Trangia ™ stove is original in that its design principle was developed specially for cooking in high winds and severe cold. The Swedish-made stove is lightweight, reliable and very compact. The smaller model is ideal for solo or two backpackers, while the larger one can easily cope with a camping group of three to four. The stove packs inside an aluminum two-pan set, complete with windshield, lids and burner and a strap to hold it all together. Trangia stoves burn denatured alcohol, which is cheap, readily available and can be carried in Trangia's purpose-made lightweight plastic fuel bottles. The stove can also run on bottled gas with a gas burner accessory. Its great advantage is that there are no moving parts, pipes or valves to break. Simply pour the fuel into the burner and ignite.

White gas (Naphtha/Coleman fuel) stoves are common in North America, but the fuel is not always readily available elsewhere, so many white gas stoves can be converted to burn other fuels. Multi-fuel stoves cost more than single-fuel models but if you are planning to visit several destinations, the added flexibility is worth the extra cost.

DUTCH OVENS

Dutch ovens work wonderfully on an open fire, on the grill or even on the stove back home. They are cooking pots made from cast-iron or aluminum, and are available in varying sizes from small (4 in/10 cm) to huge (24 in/60 cm). A 10–12-in (25–30 cm) oven is the best for group cooking. While classified as cooking pots they are much more versatile than most designs. The internal base can be used as a griddle and you can pile embers on top as well and use the pot as an oven by applying heat to the top and bottom. You can bake fresh bread each morning and roast meats very easily.

29

Dutch oven techniques

Baking: You need more heat from the top, so pile embers on the lid.

Boiling: All the heat needs to come from underneath.

Frying: You need heat from below only and cook directly on the bottom of the oven.

Griddle: Use the lid upside down as a griddle or skillet for great pancakes.

Roasting: For best results there should be equal heat from top and bottom.

Stewing: Most of the heat should come from below the oven with just a few embers on the lid.

Cast-iron Dutch ovens are very heavy and really only suitable for a static camp kitchen or if you come in by vehicle. Aluminum Dutch ovens are lighter and can be carried in a backpack. While they take up a lot of room, you can pack items inside to utilize the space fully. Aluminum Dutch ovens heat up more quickly and reflect heat which can lead to temperature fluctuations while cooking. Choose an oven that has three legs as the base must never be allowed to sit directly on hot embers. The legs enable it to straddle the embers so that there is no direct contact with them. Select one that has a lid with a ridge around the rim so that you can put hot embers on top without them sliding off.

It is advisable to preprepare a new Dutch oven by putting it in a preheated oven three times. The first heating drives out any trapped water. Before warming on the second and third occasion, completely cover the Dutch oven inside and out with a thin film of vegetable oil so that when baked, it forms a protective layer.

Trailside tips:

- Choose a Dutch oven that has a heavy-duty handle on the base and the lid and has three legs. The legs allow you to stand the oven in the embers without resting on them. This allows air to circulate under the oven and fan the flames.

- Dutch ovens get very hot! Thick gloves are essential and a pot gripper is useful for removing the lid. When full, slide a stout pole through the handle so that two people can lift the oven from the fire.

ESSENTIAL EQUIPMENT

As far as possible, research the conditions you are likely to experience along the way. When hiking along a long-distance trail, consider whether there will be adequate water supplies on the way or whether you will have to carry in all your water. If you plan to set up camp and then travel out each day, what facilities are available? There may be picnic benches and a barbecue pit, for instance, and you will not therefore need to take all of your own cooking equipment. What cooking methods are you undertaking? How many in your party? How is that going to affect what utensils you require? Each of these aspects will be your main considerations to ensure that you are well enough equipped.

POTS

Nesting cookware sets are like Russian dolls: they are comprised of a large pot containing three or four smaller pots. The lids of the pots are multi-functional and can be used as bowls, frying pans and even plates. Instead of pot and lid handles, one or two pot grippers are incorporated for removing lids or hot pots from the stove, and this makes the sets compact when packed. Typically these sets are made from aluminum. A variety of sizes and numbers of pots are available to suit different-size parties.

Solo campers require a set comprising:	Two people require a set that provides:	For four or more people, you need:
1 quart (950-ml) pot	1 1.5-quart (1.3-l) pot	1 1.5-quart (1.3-l) pot
1 1.5-quart (1.3-l) pot	1 2.5-quart (2.3-l) pot	1 2-quart (1.9-l) pot
2 lids become 2 frying pans, bowls or plates	2 lids become 2 frying pans, bowls or plates	1 2.5-quart (2.3-l) pot and lid
1 pot gripper	1 pot gripper	1 7.5-in (19-cm) frying pan
		2 lids become frying pan, bowls or plates
		2 pot grippers

UTENSILS

You will need plates, mugs, bowls, knives, forks and spoons and basic cooking utensils, such as a sharp knife to cut bread, fish, vegetables, even wood; a spatula; larger spoons for serving and mixing; pot gripper or holder (if not included in the pot kit). Select pot kits of the best quality you can afford — good cookware is a pleasure to use, especially under trailside conditions. Ensure all utensils are light and durable and above all, choose those you are comfortable using.

Trailside tips:

- Paint pot grippers a bright color or bind with reflective tape so that you can spot them easily.
- Film canisters make great containers to hold spices and small portions of jam and butter.

OTHER ESSENTIALS

Aluminum foil has countless uses on the trail. Use it to wrap food that can be dropped in to the hot embers to cook. Make a frame from wooden twigs and branches and completely cover it with foil to make a griddle. Use foil as a heat reflector or to line the base of a Dutch oven to make it easier to clean. Use it to wrap left-over food. In an emergency you can even wrap yourself in foil to keep warm or signal for help.

Plastic bags Always carry several plastic bags of different sizes. Heavy-duty freezer bags and zip-lock bags are best. They weigh almost nothing yet are worth their weight in gold. Use them to mix food ingredients, marinate dishes, collect water, to pack food, trash and a host of other things. You can even crack eggs into a plastic bag, add salt and pepper, and then suspend it in the coffee pot. As the coffee begins to heat up, so it cooks the eggs.

Pack ingredients for breakfasts, lunches and dinners separately into clearly labeled plastic bags, and then make up one large bag for each day away. The large bag contains all the food needed for that day, and means you don't have to disturb another day's rations until required.

Water carriers Choose from collapsible plastic water containers with screw-tops, plastic and fabric collapsible buckets, and any number of water bottles of different shapes and sizes. You must take a water carrier, but cooking pots and even hats can be used to collect small quantities of water.

Collected natural water must be sterilized. Even water from high altitude may be contaminated so don't take chances. Either use purification tablets or bring water to a boil, and boil for at least a further minute. Boiling for longer than this is not necessary and wastes fuel, and if you are using the water for cooking, the normal cooking process should be enough to kill any bugs. Carry a personal water bottle and replenish it whenever you get the opportunity, adding purification tablets if necessary.

Matches Buy several boxes of windproof, waterproof matches and make sure each member of the party has a box or two. Wrap the boxes in plastic bags for added waterproof protection. Cigarette lighters that are designed to ignite in windy weather are also useful.

Emergency kit Your kit should be contained in a tin and include the following: waterproof matches and/or a flint and steel for lighting fires; a couple of tea and coffee bags; chocolate; razor blades; mini flashlight; candle; water purification tablets; safety pins; needle and thread (for repairs, fishing or sutures); tweezers; antiseptic; fish hooks; whistle; and a second compass. Check your kit before each trip — hopefully it will only be the chocolate that needs replacing.

CLEARING AND DISPOSAL

If there is running water nearby, gather it into a container to wash dirty dishes, using biodegradable soap or better, by scrubbing with a handful of grass and sand. Never leave dirty dishes out because they will attract unwelcome guests. Dispose of the dirty dish water away from a lake or stream.

Always clean up the site to leave no trace you were ever there. Pick up any litter and pack in bags for carrying out. Clear up any spillages, dismantle any fire walls and scatter fire ash and any unburned wood over as wide an area as possible. Try to return the site to the condition it was in when you arrived. Pack up all your equipment and possessions. Then check thoroughly around the campsite to make sure any fire ash is totally extinguished and that you have not left anything behind. Do a final walk round to double check you have everything.

MAKING THE MOST OF SERENDIPITY

Whether you are running low on food because you've gobbled up your supplies more quickly that anticipated or you simply want a change of fare, there is no reason to go hungry on the trail, at least in some types of terrain. In lake country or beside the ocean, there may be fish, crustaceans and edible seaweeds available. Indeed, there is nothing more delicious than fresh-caught fish cooked on an open fire.

FISH FOR SUPPER

Whenever you go on the trail, always carry a couple of fish hooks and some line in your emergency kit (see page 35). Cut a suitable branch for a rod, attach the line and hook and see what you can land. You will need to bait the hook, so dig down for a juicy worm, check foliage for insect larvae or peel back some tree bark to find maggots or grubs. If wood branches are difficult to find, fish simply using a baited line secured on the riverbank or lake edge with the baited end trailing in the water. Set up a number of lines and check them frequently to see if you have a bite.

To prepare a fish for cooking, place it on its side, slice open down the belly, from the gills to the tail, and scrape out all internal organs. Wash the internal cavity thoroughly and cut off the fins. Then cut into the spine until you touch the backbone and slice the blade down either side of the backbone, filleting the meat away from the bones.

Cook your catch by skewering it onto a stick and roasting it over the fire — as it cooks it can fall apart into the fire so this method is only effective if your fish is a sizeable catch. Alternatively, wrap it in foil and bury the package in the embers of the fire or poach it in water in a pot or skillet. The last method has the benefit that you can use the liquid as a sauce, adding whatever natural ingredients you can find, such as nuts, leaves, wild garlic or anything else that provides a nutritious, if unusual, meal!

FORAGING FOR SURVIVAL

The most innocent trip can turn into a disaster. What happens if you get separated from the rest of your group? And they have all the food? Hopefully, you and they will back-track. But if you don't know the way back, you will have to fall back on your survival skills to make it home safely. How you forage for food will depend on what terrain you are in and at what time of the year it is. Water is the most critical requirement. An adult can live for three or four weeks without food but will perish after just a few days without water.

If you have to forage for food, put aside squeamishness because you won't have the luxury to decide what you would rather not put in your mouth! Many insects and grubs are edible, raw or cooked, and packed with protein. Young shoots, berries, fruits and roots of many plants are not only edible but tasty too. While some fungi are delicious, you must positively identify the species. Many fungi are not only disgusting to taste, but more importantly utterly deadly. Only eat fungi that you have confidently identified as safe. Always use good field guides to the region you are walking, to identify animals and plants you are likely to encounter. Obviously, survival skills required when alone in the wilderness in North America will be very different to those required in the Australian Outback. Inform yourself fully before you set out.

FINDING NATURAL WATER

The easiest way to locate a water source is to look at a map for a nearby stream, lake or geological feature where water might collect. If you are in a hilly or mountainous region, follow valleys down to look for springs, pools or streams. If vegetation becomes lush, water must be nearby. In spring, many trees contain water with high sugar content. If there is snow and you have a stove, start with a small amount of snow in the pot and melt it handful by handful. This is the most effective way to produce water from snow. Break ice on streams and lakes to find running water. You should boil melted ice well to purify it.

PURIFYING WATER

Even when water looks clean enough to drink there may be bugs lurking so it does pay to take basic precautions. To cleanse any natural water you collect, bring it to a boil and boil it for a full minute. Alternatively, add purification tablets according to the instructions on the packaging.

A third method is to use a water filter. The Katadyn Hiker Water Filter weighs only 11 oz (312 g) and can yield up to 200 gallons (755 l) of potable water before the filter needs replacing. You simply place one end of a plastic tube in the water and then pump it through the filter into your container. If scooping up larger amounts of water, let it stand for between 30 minutes and an hour to allow silt and sand to settle in the bottom of the container and then filter into another container. Don't disturb the silt.

Filter straws, just a little larger than a conventional straw, can be used to suck up small pools of water. Once the filter is full, no more water can be produced. This means that you can safely use it to get potable water from even the foulest-looking sources.

AVOID FOODS THAT

+ You don't recognize or cannot identify from field guides.
+ Smell bad or are decaying.
+ Have a three-leafed growth pattern.
+ Are overripe or contain a milky sap.
+ Contain seeds in a pod.
+ Smell of almonds — they may contain cyanide compounds.
+ Are growing in, or close to, polluted water.

CHAPTER THREE

GET SET . . . PACK

The average vacationer returns from a trip having worn only two thirds of the clothes taken away. The rest were, in every sense, excess baggage. When you are packing in readiness for backpacking over several days, you must pack only what you truly need because a) you are going to have to carry it all the way throughout the day, there and back; and b) space is limited. Experienced backpackers know exactly what they need and will assemble the most efficient and the lightest kit they can.

We have friends who drill holes in the handles of their toothbrush to reduce weight. They take paperback books and each day use the pages they have read to light the fire. You don't need to go to these extremes to put together a pack that is light yet still contains everything you will need to have both a comfortable and enjoyable trip. Just think very carefully about how much you will really use each item that you are considering putting into your pack.

PACK LIGHT

Thanks to modern technology, a pack containing all your needs for a four-day trip weighs today about half as much as it might have 20 years ago. A pack containing tent, sleeping bag and mat, stove, fuel, water, food, clothes, wet-weather gear and other essentials need weigh no more than 30 pounds (13.5 kg). With the lightest gear available you can cut this down even further.

A three-season sleeping bag weighing 2 pounds (1 kg), when used in conjunction with an all-weather bivouac bag, will provide a 3-pound (1.3-kg) combo that will keep you alive in the most extreme conditions — and you won't even need a tent.

If you want the luxury of a tent, you can get a three-season, two-person tent weighing around 4 pounds (1.8 kg). Add to that a lightweight stove, fuel, a set of cooking pots, a collapsible plastic bucket, flashlight, first-aid and emergency kit, and you have all the main camping needs weighing at little more than 10 pounds (4.5 kg). All of this has to go into your pack, together with wet-weather gear, clothing, food and whatever else you want to take on the trail.

Stuff sacks come in different sizes and it is useful to have several, in different colors, for wet-weather gear, clothing, sleeping bag and so on. Stuff sacks are effective because once a sack is filled, and all the air is pressed out, it becomes as compressed as possible, and you can then secure it so that the sack cannot expand. Even a bulky sleeping bag can be compressed to a quarter of its size in this way. It will not reduce the weight, but it does mean you can carry more and everything is kept orderly, which makes life a lot easier on the trail.

HOW MUCH FOOD TO TAKE?

If you are on the trail for just one day or a weekend, you can follow the sort of diet that you would at home. The extra energy expended will burn off some surplus (unless you are super fit). However, if you are planning to be out for several days or even weeks, you will need to adjust your diet accordingly because you will want a more energy-efficient carlorie-rich diet.

There are several ways to calculate how much food you will need — calories required per person, weight of food per person and so on — but the easiest method is to create a meal plan.

We work out what makes a nutritious menu that provides three hearty meals a day; we then add enough snacks and treats to ensure that we get the right mix of nutrients and the required number of calories. Several days before you set out write out your menu plan. Here's an example:

Breakfast · Lunch · Dinner · Snacks/Others	
Day 1	Bacon and eggs on a bagel · Swedish apple soup · Vegetarian chili · Pineapple sundae · Trail mix/energy bars
Day 2	Banana pancakes · Pita pizza · Goulash · Coconut surprise · Trail mix/energy bars
Day 3	Fruit treat · Summa' soup · Lemon couscous · Chocolate fondue · Trail mix/energy bars
Day 4	Breakfast casserole · No-pot stew · Pasta Alfredo · Berries galore · Trail mix/energy bars

Menu planning helps focus on the perishable foods and identifies meal-by-meal what you need to prepare in advance, and what ingredients you need to have as staples at camp.

Draw up a list of all the ingredients required. Quantities will, of course, be determined by how many people are in the group. Check off any you already have in the cupboard, but do not accidentally omit them at packing.

LABELING THE FOOD

When you are ready to pack, lay out all the food items required. Pack the ingredients for each meal into plastic "meal bags." For example, a breakfast bag may contain just two or three ingredient bags. A dinner bag may contain up to five ingredient bags. Then pack them all into a "day bag," which contains all the rations needed for one day's meals. "Day bags" can be distributed between members of the group. For example, if there are four people out for four days, they each carry one day's bag. Pack "kitchen bags" of herbs, sauces, seasonings, and so on. Trail mixes, energy bars can be packed separately so that each member carries their own trail mix ration for the trip.

Color-code meal bags. For example, green labels for breakfast, red for lunch and blue for dinner. Write on each meal bag label what it contains and slip the day's menu plan into its respective day bag. If you are trying a new recipe, pack the instructions as well!

BACKPACKERS' PROVISIONS

Foods that keep well on the trail and form the basis for many trailside recipes include:

Pantry staples		No-cook instants
Coffee and tea bags (or ground coffee)	Peanut butter	Cheese (hard)
Cocoa/hot chocolate drinks	Marshmallows	Potato chips
Sugar/sweetener	Sauces (packets, dehydrated and preferably homemade)	Energy and granola bars
Seasoning, spices and herbs	Dehydrated fruit, vegetables and meats	Fruit slices (dehydrated)
Noodles, pasta, rice	Dried beans, pulses and lentils	Dried meats such as jerky, salami, pepperoni
Powdered eggs and milk	Homemade dehydrated soups, stews and casseroles	Nuts
Margarine (or clarified butter) and vegetable oil	Cake mixes	Trail mixes
Instant mashed potatoes	Flour	
Oatmeal/homemade cereal mixes (with added nuts, dried fruit and dried milk)		
Parmesan (grated)		
Stock cubes/extracts		

Breads and crackers		Luxuries
Pita bread (lasts well on the trail and packs tightly)	Bake fresh bread every other day (the ingredients weigh less to carry in than the finished product)	Chocolate chips (chocolate chip pancakes for breakfast!)
Bagels (can be toasted if they start to get stale)		Chocolate bars
Dry crackers and crisp breads (to eat with cheese or soup)		Cans of pâté and/or caviar
		(And your heart's desires — provided you are willing to carry it!)

Essential backpack items

Tent and sleeping gear

Stove and fuel (separate from food)

Food

Utensils

First-aid kit including tweezers

Compass

Emergency kit

Flashlight

ID (personal identification)

Knife — multi-blade (sharp blade, scissors, corkscrew, mini saw, can opener)

Map

Matches

Clothing

Sandals or running shoes (to slip into when the boots come off)

Socks and sock liners

Hat

Sewing kit (for basic repairs, emergency sutures)

Wet-weather gear

Water bottle

Additional items for longer trips

Fire lighter or flint and steel

Headlamp or lantern

Extra batteries for flashlight

Washing kit, towel and other personal requirements

Toilet paper

Emergency blanket or lightweight tarpaulin

Nylon rope — 30 feet (10 m)

Small roll of duct tape

Small trowel or very lightweight folding shovel (for digging a latrine)

Water purification tablets/filter

Aluminum foil

MORE FOOD!

Seasonal requirements

Gloves

Insect repellant

Lip balm

Sunglasses

Sunscreen

Pack cover (a waterproof that slips over your pack to protect it from the rain)

Small hatchet/folding saw (for chopping firewood)

Weather radio (lightweight and tuned to receive the forecast for the area)

Optional items, depending on your interests

Binoculars (compact)

Camera (spare batteries and/or film)

Playing cards

Field guides

Fishing line and hooks

Wet wipes

Journey log and pen

Paperback/magazines (excellent tinder when lighting fires)

45

CAMPSITE COMFORTS — IF CONVEYED BY VEHICLE

When you are not carrying everything on your back, but setting up a base or trailside campsite, the following items go beyond the basic essentials, but will give camp life that extra degree of gastronomy and comfort:

Kitchen items

Coffeepot	Dishwashing bowl	Paper towels
Cooler	Griddle	Plastic wrap
Corkscrew	Grill and charcoal	Skillet
Cutting board	Measuring cup	Spatulas and spoons
Dish cloths	Mixing bowls	Water jugs

Overnight comforts

Air mattresses (and pump)	Camp chairs and table	Pillows
Axe	Canopy	Portable chemical toilet
Broom (small)	Fire extinguisher	Shower (solar showers are
Camp beds	Mallet	fun if you have water!)

Trailside tips:

- If you are heading out on a four-day trip, carry an extra bag containing two main meals, mostly of dehydrated foods. If you are delayed for any reason, you have some back-up food. If it's not needed, you can eat it up back at home.

- Every time you close up a bag, squeeze as much air out as possible, so that it takes up less room.

- Don't take foods that will spoil quickly unless you plan to eat them in the first day or two. Avoid soft cheeses, mayonnaise, butter, fresh eggs and fresh milk.

- Repack the contents of cans into plastic bags.

- As each day's rations are consumed, the empty bags and any trash can be transferred to a "garbage bag" that comes home with you.

SAMPLE MENUS AND PACK LISTS

One-day hike

- **Trail bread** (p. 116) — French bread, pâté and a selection of hard and soft cheese (Cheddar and Brie). Prepared, sliced fruit. Eat separately or mix in a pot of yogurt
- **Pita pizza** (p. 81) • **Trail granola** (p. 52) Split the mix into two packets – one for morning and one after lunch • Snacks (p. 53–58)

Packing checklist for one person on a one-day hike

Water	2 bread rolls	Apple
4 tea or coffee bags	4 oz/110 g cheese	Trail mix
Soup for lunch	Slices of salami	Energy bar/chocolate bar

Weekend (two-day) hike

Day 1 Crusty bread with • **Black bean spread** (p. 84), spread on **crispbread** or **bread** (p. 116) • **Vegetarian chili** (p. 132) prepared ahead to serve with rice • **Banana boats** (p. 133).

Day 2 • Bacon and eggs on a bagel (p. 71) • **Swedish apple soup** (p. 79) • Trail mix and **energy bars** (p. 52–58)

Packing checklist for two people on a two-day hike

Staples:
Water
8 tea or coffee bags
Margarine (in a tube)
Powdered milk
Sugar/sweeteners
Salt and pepper
Cookies (as desired)

Breakfast:
4 large, thin, precooked slices bacon
4 eggs or egg powder equivalent
2 bagels

Lunches:
Black bean spread (p. 84)
Swedish apple soup (p. 79)
Loaf of crusty bread

Dinners:
Vegetarian chili (p. 132)
1 cup/250 ml rice
2 bananas
4 marshmallows
4 tbsp chocolate chips

Trail mix/snacks:
Trail granola (p. 52)
4 energy bars (pp. 52–58)

Four-day hike

Day 1 • No-pot stew (p. 88) • Lentil chili (p. 94) • Fruit grill (p. 131)

Day 2 • Fruit treat (p. 66) • Apple and turkey stirfry (p. 89) • Lemon couscous with chicken (p. 101) • Mint chocolate pots (p. 137)

Day 3 French toast (p. 72)• Bacon and Cheddar spread on crackers (p. 85) • Banana bread (p. 122) • Goulash (p. 130) • Pineapple sundae (p. 127)

Day 4 • Banana pancakes (p. 67) • Summa' soup (p. 80)

Packing checklist for four people on a four-day hike

Staples:
Water
64 coffee or tea bags
Container of powdered milk
Sugar or sweeteners
Salt and pepper
Butter or margarine
Vegetable oil
Dried herbs
Cookies

Breakfasts:
Fruit treat (p. 66)
8 thick slices bread
6 eggs or egg powder
Vanilla extract
2 cups/500 ml flour
1 tsp baking powder
1 banana

Lunches:
2 medium potatoes ✿
3 onions ✿
6 carrots ✿
1 green bell pepper ✿
4 cloves garlic
Soy sauce

Worcestershire sauce
Cornstarch
1/2 cup/125 ml apple juice
1 lb/450 g turkey breast ✿
1 cup/250 ml snow peas ✿
4 cups/1,000 ml rice
4 stock cubes
1/2 cup/125 ml dried vegetables
5 slices bacon
1 cup/250 ml grated Cheddar cheese
Salad dressing
Crackers

Dinners and snacks:
2 cloves garlic
2 onions ✿
1 cup/250 ml dried lentils
1 cup/250 ml bulgur wheat
3 potatoes ✿
8 stock cubes
1 can chopped tomatoes
Chili powder
Ground cumin
1 lb /450 g diced chicken ✿

1 lemon
1 cup/250 ml couscous
Dried herbs
1 lb/450 g ground beef ✿
1 green bell pepper ✿
2 stalks celery ✿
1 tbsp paprika
1/2 cup/125 ml sour cream
2 cups/500 ml noodles
2 lbs/1 kg assorted fruit ✿
15 marshmallows
13/4 cup/250 ml choc chips
1 cup/250 ml milk
1 egg
1/3 cup/75 ml cocoa
1/4 cup/50 ml flour
1 pineapple
2 oranges
1 banana
8 oz/225 g strawberries
2 tbsp crystalized ginger
2 cups/500 ml plain yogurt
25 energy bars
16 x 2-cup/475-ml bags trail granola (p. 52)

Trail mixes, boosters & drinks

Trail mixes are essential supplies on the trail to keep energy levels high, especially if you are walking over rough terrain and carrying a heavy pack, and trail mixes of nuts, raisins and dried fruits provide a quick energy boost. Energy bars are also important both as carb-loaders and morale boosters.

Drinks are equally crucial to keep the body well hydrated, and refuelled with nutrients. If it is chilly, they provide warmth and there is no better feeling than sitting around a campfire under the stars, having enjoyed a great dinner, with a warm drink in your hand.

Trail granola

Enjoy this granola for breakfast or nibble it along the trail. Like all trail mixes, you can add your favorite ingredients to make it even more appetizing. Makes enough for breakfast for two people plus leftovers to supply trail mix for two people for two days.

Makes **8** portions　Prep. time: **10** mins　Cooking time: **25** mins

8 tbsp/120 ml	**margarine**
1/2 cup/125 ml	**brown sugar**
1 tbsp/15 ml	**cinnamon**
4 cups/1,000 ml	**rolled oats**
2 cups/500 ml	**bulgur**
1 cup/250 ml	**wheat germ**
1/2 cup/125 ml	**sesame seeds**
1 cup/250 ml	**mixed raisins and banana slices**

At home:

Preheat the oven to 450°F/230°C. In a pan over a medium heat, melt the margarine and brown sugar and bring to a boil, stirring continuously. Remove from the heat and stir in the cinnamon. Add the oats, bulgur, wheat germ and sesame seeds and stir until everything is well combined.

Empty out the mixture on to a 9 x 13-in/23 x 33-cm baking tray and spread evenly. Bake in the oven for about 25 minutes.

Remove from the oven and allow to cool on the tray. Mix in the raisins and banana slices and bag as required.

Quick energy bar

This is another tasty trailside treat that will give you a fast energy burst if you are feeling weary and still have a few miles to go before stopping for the night. It also freezes well.

Makes **18** bars   Prep. time: **10** mins   Cooking time: **20** mins

4 tbsp/60 ml	**margarine**
1 cup/250 ml	**crushed graham crackers**
1 cup/250 ml	**shredded coconut**
2 cups/500 ml	**chocolate chips**
14-oz /425-ml	**can condensed milk**
1 cup/250 ml	**chopped walnuts**
3/4 cup/175 ml	**rolled oats**

At home:

Preheat the oven to 350°F/180°C. Place the margarine on a 9 x 13-in/23 x 33-cm baking tray and melt the margarine in the oven for 1 minute. Remove the tray from the oven. Spread a layer of crushed graham crackers over the tray.

Cover this layer with a layer of shredded coconut.

Cover with a layer of chocolate chips.

Finally, pour the condensed milk over.

Bake for about 20 minutes until golden brown.

Remove from the oven and add the walnuts and the rolled oats, gently pressing them into the mixture before it cools. Allow to cool on the tray and cut the mixture into individual bars. Pack individually in foil. Eat within a week or so, or freeze until required.

Granny's granola bars

Marshmallows are the key ingredient here. They are a great comfort food. They are also light, they keep well and you can eat them on the trail. Try cooking with them as below, or roasting them on sticks around the campfire.

Makes **12** bars   Prep. time: **10** mins

3 tbsp/45 ml	margarine
10-oz/280-g	package marshmallows
2 cups/500 ml	mixed nuts and raisins
2 cups/500 ml	corn flakes or rice cereal
2 cups/500 ml	granola

At home:

In a large pan, melt the margarine and slowly add the marshmallows. Heat very gently until the mixture is completely melted. Stir in the nuts, raisins, cereal and granola and combine all the ingredients. Pour onto a 9 x 13-in/23 x 33-cm baking tray and spread the mixture evenly. Allow to stand for 15 minutes and cut into bars. Wrap each bar individually. These bars are best eaten within four days.

Carrot and date bar

A lovely combination of flavors, tastes and textures and packed with goodness.
When cooking with honey, first rub a film of oil on your spoon to prevent the honey
sticking — it will slide off easily. Another method is to dip your spoon or cup
into flour first.

Makes **16** bars   Prep. time: **15** mins   Cooking time: **30** mins

1 cup/250 ml	**whole wheat flour**
1 tsp/5 ml	**baking powder**
1/2 tsp/2 ml	**salt**
2	**eggs**
1/2 cup/125 ml	**honey**
1 cup/250 ml	**chopped dates**
1 cup/250 ml	**finely shredded carrot**
1/2 cup/125 ml	**chopped walnuts**

At home:

Preheat the oven to 350°F/180°C. Grease a 9 x 9-in/23 x 23-cm baking tray. In a large
bowl, mix the flour, baking powder and salt. In a second bowl beat the eggs and honey
together. Then slowly add the flour mix and blend well.

Add the dates, carrot and nuts and mix well. Spoon the mixture onto the baking tray
and spread evenly. Bake for 30 minutes or until golden brown.

Remove from the oven and allow to cool on the tray before cutting into bars. Pack in
airtight bags and store in a cool place if you plan to eat them within a few days,
otherwise store in the refrigerator until required.

Fruit balls

If you need a quick energy fix or just want a mouthful of flavor, pop in a fruit ball. You can use any dried fruits, although apricots work really well because of their high sugar content.

Makes **16**   Prep. time: **10** mins

3/4 cup/175 ml	**dried apricots or other dried fruit**
1 cup/250 ml	**shredded coconut**
1/2 cup/125 ml	**condensed milk**
2 tbsp/30 ml	**confectioner's sugar**

At home:
In a large bowl, mix the fruit and coconut. Pour in the milk and blend well. Shape into balls (about 16) and roll in the sugar to coat. Pack in airtight bags.

Chocolate kickers

If you start to flag toward the end of the day, pop one of these energy-packed balls into your mouth and you'll find you've got a new spring in your step. A delicious treat that can be made before you leave or at camp.

Makes **15** bite-size balls   Prep. time: **15** mins

1 cup/250 ml	**confectioner's sugar**
1 cup/250 ml	**crunchy peanut butter**
1 cup/250 ml	**dark or semi-sweet chocolate chips**
1/2 cup/125 ml	**powdered milk**
2 tbsp/30 ml	**water**

At home:
Mix all the ingredients together in a large bowl and shape into bite-size balls. Allow to stand for 15 minutes and pack into airtight bags.

Nutty oatmeal cookies

This is an easy way to make cookies on the trail without having to do any cooking.
All you have to do is a little mixing and boil some water.

Makes **12**   Prep. time: **10** mins

2 tbsp/30 ml	**butter or margarine**
1/4 cup/50 ml	**chocolate milk powder**
1 1/2 cups/375 ml	**rolled oats**
2 tbsp/30 ml	**powdered milk**
pinch	**salt**
3 tbsp/45 ml	**peanut butter**
1/3 cup/75 ml	**sugar**

At home:

Heat 1/4 cup/50 ml water in a large pan. Add the butter and chocolate milk powder and
bring to a boil. Add all the remaining ingredients except the sugar and mix well.
Shape the mixture into balls (about 12), flatten them onto a tray and sprinkle with
sugar. Pack in airtight bags and store in a cool, dark place. They will keep for about a
week. If you want to keep them longer, they will need to be refrigerated.

Pam's nuts (we know that!)

A delicious and nutritious nutty snack that is great for on-the-move trail food — or when watching TV back home.

Serves **2**   Prep. time: **10** mins   Cooking time: **20** mins

1 tbsp/15 ml	**salt**
1/2 tsp/2 ml	**cayenne pepper**
1/2 tsp/2 ml	**white pepper**
1/2 tsp/2 ml	**ground nutmeg**
1/2 tsp/2 ml	**ground allspice**
4 cups/1,000 ml	**assorted unsalted, shelled nuts (such as peanuts, cashews, pecans, walnut pieces, almonds)**
1/2 stick/60 ml	**butter**
1/2 cup/125 ml	**maple syrup, light molasses or treacle**

At home:

Preheat the oven to 350ºF/180ºC. Place all the seasonings in a large bowl, add the nuts and mix to combine.

In a pan over a medium heat, melt the butter and add it to the mixture. Stir all the ingredients until they are well combined.

Place the mixture on a 9 x 13-in/23 x 33-cm baking tray and bake in the oven until roasted, about 10 minutes.

Stir occasionally to prevent sticking.

Put the roasted nuts back into the bowl and add the maple syrup and stir to coat the nuts. Return the mixture to the baking tray and bake for a further 10 minutes, until the nuts have a darkish, glazed appearance.

Allow to cool and then pack into airtight containers.

Fruit cocktail

A thirst-quenching drink any time. Great for breakfast, lunch or dinner and a great reviver at the end of a long day on the trail.

Serves 4

1 cup/250 ml	**orange juice**
1 cup/250 ml	**pineapple juice**
1 cup/250 ml	**grapefruit juice**
1 cup/250 ml	**cranberry juice**

Simply combine all the juices and bottle. Shake well before serving.
Keep in an airtight container and this drink will be good for several days.

Lemonade

A wonderfully refreshing drink that can be sweetened to suit your taste. This lemonade is at its best chilled. Simply place in a seal-tight container and immerse in cool water or, if you have a cooler, even better. However, it's also soothingly refreshing when served warm.

Serves 4

1 cup/250 ml	**lemon juice**
4 tsp/20 ml	**sugar**
4 cups/1 l	**water**

Combine the lemon juice with the sugar in a large sealed container and stir until the sugar is dissolved. Add the water, stir and serve.

Spicy hot chocolate

This is a really decadent hot drink for those special moments when life under canvas needs spicing up and for when you need a sugar hit. This is the perfect drink for chocaholics.

Serves 6   Prep./cooking time: 10 mins

2 x 4-oz/110-g	**bars dark or milk chocolate**
4 cups/1 l	**water**
1¼ cups/300 ml	**condensed milk**
pinch	**cayenne pepper**
½ tsp/2 ml	**cinnamon**

Break the chocolate into small pieces. Boil the water in a pan and add the chocolate and milk. Stir over a medium heat until all the chocolate has melted. Add the cayenne. Serve sprinkled with cinnamon.

Spiced tea

Tea is always invigorating and this spiced-up version is even more refreshing, especially at the end of a long, tiring day.

Serves 8

½ cup/125 ml	**sugar**
8	**tea bags**
6	**cloves**
1	**cinnamon stick**
	strips of orange rind

In a pan over a gentle heat, melt the sugar in ¾ cup /175 ml water to produce a syrup. Make up the tea in 4 cups/1 l water.
Remove the sugar syrup from the heat and add the cloves, cinnamon stick and orange rind. Pour into the hot tea, stir and serve piping hot.

Rose hip tea

Rose hips (the fruit of the rose) produce a very delicate and refreshing flavor and they can be collected from hedgerows and gardens at the end of the summer.

1/3 cup/75 ml   fresh rose hips per cup

Boil the water, remove from the heat and add the rose hips. Steep for 15 to 20 minutes. Serve with honey to sweeten, if desired.

Beef tea

A quick, warming and nutritious pick-me-up anywhere, anytime.

Add boiling water to mugs containing 2 teaspoons each of Marmite, Bovril, Vegemite or 2 beef bouillion cubes.

Ginger water

Ginger water is a wonderful thirst-quencher, as well as a good remedy for upset stomachs and nausea. It is best to use fresh ginger, peeled and grated — fresh ginger keeps for several days so it is useful on the trail for a number of recipes.

Serves 6

4-in/10-cm   piece fresh ginger, peeled and grated
3/4 cup/175 ml   sugar
4 cups/1 l   water
1   orange, peeled and sliced

Mix the grated ginger, sugar and water together in a sealed container and leave to stand for 6 hours. Immerse the container in a cold-water stream or lake, as this drink is best served chilled. To serve, strain to remove the pulp and ginger, and pour into mugs. Decorate with orange slices.

Chocolate coffee

This is the perfect drink for chocolate and caffeine addicts. Drink it warm and it makes a great after-dinner drink or nightcap. Drink it cold and it is perfect at lunch on a hot summer's day. Two or three black cherries added to the mug is a special treat.

Serves 2

2 cups/500 ml	**water**
2 tbsp/30 ml	**fresh coffee grounds**
4-oz/110-g	**bar dark chocolate, broken into pieces**

Boil the water in a pan, add the coffee grounds and stir. Remove from the heat and add the chocolate, piece by piece, and stir until melted.
Pour into mugs, using a spoon to hold back the coffee grounds.

Camp coffee

The first thing the first person to wake up should do is put on the coffee.

One of the quickest, most efficient and delicious ways to make a large pot of camp coffee is to boil the water in a big pot for 5 minutes.

Add 1 tsp coffee per cup, boil it up again for 2 to 3 more minutes, then take the pot off the heat and leave it to stand for 1 minute.

Dribble half a cup cold water along the surface, tap the pot repeatedly with a metal utensil for about 30 seconds to make the grounds sink to the bottom. Let the coffee settle for another minute, and then pour hot steaming coffee gently from the top.

Breakfasts

Breakfast is the most important meal of the day because it packs in the fuel you will need on the trail. We are also of the firm belief that it should be an enjoyable meal. There is no reason why you should eat a bowl of oatmeal every day, no matter how good this may be for you. Be adventurous and you'll be amazed by what you can create.

Oatmeal surprise

Add different ingredients whenever you serve this nutritious bowl. Apart from using a range of fruits, both dried and fresh, you can use different toppings — honey, syrup and one of our favorite combinations — cranberry and brown sugar.

Serves **4**   Prep. time: **5** mins   Cooking time: less than **5** mins

3 cups/750 ml	**milk or reconstituted powdered milk**
1¹/₂ cups/375 ml	**instant oatmeal**
1 cup/250 ml	**dried cranberries**
1 tsp/5 ml	**brown sugar**
pinch	**cinnamon**

At camp:

Bring the milk to a boil in a large pan. Add the oatmeal and cook for a further minute, stirring occasionally. Remove from the heat, add the cranberries and brown sugar and mix well. Serve with a sprinkling of cinnamon.

Fruit treat

Serves **2**   Prep. time: **2** mins   Cooking time: **3–4** mins

¹/₂ cup/125 ml	**chopped dried apricots**
3 cups/750 ml	**water**
¹/₂ cup/125 ml	**raisins**
¹/₂ tsp/2 ml	**salt**
1 cup/250 ml	**powdered milk**
8-oz/225-g	**can rice pudding**
¹/₄ cup/50 ml	**brown sugar**

At camp:

Place the apricots and water in a pan and bring to a boil. Gradually stir in the remaining ingredients, bring back to a boil and cook for 1 minute, stirring frequently. Remove from the heat, cover with a lid and stand for 5 minutes, then pour into bowls to serve.

Banana pancakes

This recipe is quick and easy to prepare and provides a delicious, healthy, energy-packed breakfast. You can substitute other fruits for the bananas.

Serves 6 (2 pancakes each) Prep. time: 5 mins
Cooking time: 10–15 mins for the complete batch

2 cups/500 ml	all-purpose flour
1 tsp/5 ml	salt
2 tbsp/30 ml	sugar
1 tsp/5 ml	baking soda
2	eggs or egg powder equivalent
2 cups/500 ml	milk or reconstituted powdered milk
1/2 stick/60 ml	butter
1	banana, finely sliced
1 tbsp/15 ml	vegetable oil

At camp:

In a large bowl, mix together the flour, salt, sugar and baking soda. In a smaller bowl, mix the eggs, milk and butter. Blend in the dry mixture to form a batter. Gradually add the sliced banana to the mix.

Heat a skillet over a medium heat, add a little oil to prevent sticking, and pour in about 2 tablespoons of batter for each pancake. Serve with jams, jellies or other preserves.

Scrambled eggs 'n' coffee

Cook your eggs while you make your coffee. It's simple and economical on fuel and time. When your eggs are cooked, place them on to a plate and pour a cup of coffee. This is the fastest way to cook breakfast and the best thing about it is that it makes great, fluffy scrambled eggs.

Serves **2**   Prep. time: **5** mins   Cooking time: **10** mins

4	**eggs or egg powder equivalent**
3 tbsp/45 ml	**milk or reconstituted powdered milk**
	salt and pepper, to taste

At camp:

Boil water in a pan or coffee pot. Crack the eggs into a plastic bag, add the milk and season to taste.

Pop the bag into the boiling water for a few minutes and then remove and check your eggs. If the eggs look cooked i.e., there is no liquid in the bag, keep the bag closed and use your fingers to scramble them through the bag. Open the bag and serve.

You could add a little cheese to the eggs in the initial mix or sprinkle some on the eggs on the plate.

Country no-crust quiche

If you plan a lazy morning and leisurely breakfast, then you can find things to do around the campsite while this quiche cooks in the Dutch oven — it will be worth the wait and you can finish it off cold for lunch.

Serves 6   Prep. time: 10 mins   Cooking time: 30–45 mins

1 tbsp/15 ml	butter
1 tbsp/15 ml	all-purpose flour
1 cup/250 ml	grated cheese (Cheddar or Gruyere)
4	large eggs or egg powder equivalent
1 1/2 cups/375 ml	milk or light cream
1 tbsp/15 ml	chopped herbs (fresh or dried)
1/2 tsp/2 ml	salt
pinch	nutmeg
pinch	pepper

At camp:

Line a Dutch oven with foil and grease with butter. Bring to a medium heat.

Put the flour in a bag, add the cheese and toss to coat in the flour. In a bowl, beat the eggs and add the milk, herbs, salt, nutmeg and pepper.

Add the coated cheese to the egg mixture, and pour into the Dutch oven.

Bake until set. Remove from the oven, allow to rest for 10 minutes then slice and serve.

Omelet in a bag

Serves 1   Prep. time: 2 mins   Cooking time: less than 5 mins

2	eggs
1 tbsp/15 ml	grated cheese
❄ 1 tbsp/15 ml	diced ham, optional
❄ 1 tbsp/15 ml	diced peppers, optional
❄ 1 tbsp/15 ml	diced tomatoes, optional
	salt and pepper, to taste

At camp:

Set a large pan of water to boil. Crack the eggs into a large, sealable plastic bag and add the remaining ingredients. Seal the bag and then squish it with your fingers so that the contents are well mixed. Place the bag in the pot of boiling water and cook for 3 or 4 minutes, stirring occasionally. The eggs are done when there is no longer any liquid in the bag. Open the bag and slip the omelet onto a plate.

Bacon and eggs on a bagel

Bacon keeps well on the trail if precooked and sealed in plastic wrap. It will last for four or five days under most conditions and can be reheated in a frying pan.

Serves 2   Prep. time: 5 mins   Cooking time: 5 mins

4	slices precooked bacon
4	eggs
3 tbsp/45 ml	milk or reconstituted powdered milk
1 tbsp/15 ml	butter or margarine
2	bagels
	salt and pepper, to taste

At camp:

Make scrambled eggs as per the instructions on page 68. Reheat the bacon and serve with the eggs on both halves of a buttered sliced bagel.

French toast

This is a very easy, tasty and filling breakfast and a great way to use up any old bread as well.

Serves **2** (3 slices each)   Prep. time: **2—3** mins   Cooking time: **15** mins

2	**eggs or egg powder equivalent**
½ cup/125 ml	**milk or reconstituted powdered milk**
3 drops	**vanilla extract**
pinch	**cinnamon, optional**
6	**thick slices white bread**
4 tbsp/60 ml	**butter or margarine**

At camp:

Break the eggs into a bowl and add the milk, vanilla and cinnamon. Dip the slices of bread into the mixture to thoroughly coat both sides.

Melt a little butter in a hot skillet. Add a slice of bread to the pan, one at a time. Cook each side for 2 to 3 minutes, until golden brown. Add more butter or margarine as needed.

Serve with jam, jelly, honey or maple syrup.

All-day breakfast

Serves **2**   Prep. time: **5** mins   Cooking time: **10** mins

✲ **6**	**sausage links or small sausages**
✲ **1**	**potato**
6	**eggs or egg powder equivalent**
3 tbsp/45 ml	**milk or reconstituted powdered milk**
✲ **1/2 cup/125 ml**	**chopped mushrooms**
1/2 cup/125 ml	**grated cheese**
	salt and pepper, to taste

At camp:

In a frying pan or skillet, fry the sausages for 10 minutes, until they are cooked through. While the sausages are cooking, peel and finely dice the potato.

When the sausages are cooked, remove them from the pan and cut into bite-size pieces. In the fat remaining in the pan, cook the diced potato until soft and golden. Beat the eggs, mix in the milk and pour the mixture over the potato. As the eggs are cooking, add the mushrooms and grated cheese, and season to taste. Serve as the cheese melts.

Breakfast casserole

This Dutch-oven breakfast is sometimes referred to as the cholesterol casserole — for obvious reasons. It does taste very good though!

Serves 4 hungry campers   Prep. time: 10 mins   Cooking time: 40 mins

1 tbsp/15 ml	butter
4	thick slices white bread
1 lb/455 g	cooked sausage patties or cooked sausage meat
1 cup/250 ml	grated Cheddar cheese
6	eggs or egg powder equivalent
2 cups/500 ml	milk or reconstituted powdered milk
1 tsp/5 ml	mustard powder
	salt, to taste

At camp:

Line a Dutch oven with foil and grease with butter. Break up the bread and form a base in the bottom of the oven. Crumble the sausage over the bread and cover with cheese. In a bowl, lightly beat the eggs, milk and mustard and season to taste. Pour this mixture over the cheese. Cover and bake for 35 to 40 minutes. As it cooks, the cheese rises to the top and forms a golden crust over a layer of eggs. Make sure it does not cook too fast and that the eggs are cooked through to your liking.

Soups, snacks & lunches

If you are enjoying a leisurely circular walk you will have the luxury of stopping for lunch and rustling something up. If you are trying to cover a set distance every day, a short stop will give you enough time to heat up some soup or tuck into a tasty snack. Either way, we hope you will find something to tempt you in the following pages.

Chickpea and pasta soup

Sometimes it is good to take a lingering and leisurely lunch and this is the ideal soup for those occasions.

Serves **4** large helpings   Prep. time: **5** mins   Cooking time: **30** mins

1 tbsp/15 ml	**olive oil**
4	**cloves garlic, minced**
1 tbsp/15 ml	**chopped fresh rosemary**
2 cups/500 ml	**chopped canned tomatoes**
2 cups/500 ml	**chicken stock**
1 cup/250 ml	**canned chickpeas**
1 cup/250 ml	**pasta (such as macaroni or fusilli)**

At camp:

Heat the oil in a large pot over a medium heat. Add the garlic and sauté gently for 3 to 4 minutes, stirring frequently to prevent the garlic from burning.

Add the rosemary and cook for a further 2 minutes. Add the tomatoes, cover and simmer for 15 minutes. Add the stock and simmer, covered, for another 10 minutes. Finally, add the chickpeas, pasta, season and cook for a further 8 to 10 minutes, until *al dente*.

Swedish apple soup

This is a thick gazpacho-type soup and it is very refreshing and convenient for lunch. It must be prepared at home and is best eaten cold.

Serves 4   Prep. time: 10 mins   Cooking time: 45 mins

6	dessert apples, peeled, cored and sliced
2	cloves
1 tbsp/15 ml	sugar
1 tbsp/15 ml	cinnamon
3/4 cup/175 ml	butter, melted
1 cup/250 ml	sugar
1 cup/250 ml	all-purpose flour
1	egg or egg powder equivalent
2–3 drops	vanilla extract
	salt, to taste

At home:

Preheat the oven to 350°F/180°C. Grease a 9-in/23-cm pie dish and build up layers of apple slices until about two-thirds full. Add the cloves and sprinkle with the sugar and cinnamon.

In a bowl, thoroughly combine the butter, cup of sugar, flour, egg, vanilla and a little salt to taste. Pour over the apples and bake for about 45 minutes. Allow to cool completely then store in airtight bags or containers.

Summa' soup

This lunch is best served toward the end of your trip and allows you to use up any leftovers — thus the name: summa' this and summa' that! Always have the basic ingredients such as beef, chicken and vegetable stock cubes, herbs and spices with you to get things going.

Serves 4   Prep. time: 5 mins   Cooking time: 10 mins

1 cup/250 ml	**diced assorted dried vegetables**
4	**stock cubes**
	dried herbs, to taste
	salt and pepper, to taste
2 cups/500 ml	**rice, noodles or couscous**

At home:
Dehydrate the vegetables and pack in an airtight bag.

At camp:
Boil 4 cups/1 l water and crumble in the stock cubes. Add the herbs and season to taste. Reduce the heat and add whatever leftover vegetables and meats are available. Use spaghetti and you have minestrone-style soup.
Use vegetable stock and add beans, noodles and leftovers to make a rich vegetable bean soup.
Use beef stock cubes, add a little milk and mushrooms plus leftovers and rice and you have a stroganoff-beef and mushroom combination.
When using leftovers, always warm them thoroughly but don't let the water boil or everything will become mushy. Simmering the contents will ensure they are hot when served and that any bacteria have been destroyed.

Pita fillings

Be adventurous when it comes to pita fillings. Here are some suggestions to brighten a pita sandwich.

At camp:

Mix together some diced, cooked chicken breast, finely sliced onion and 1 tsp of salsa to make a Mexican pita.

Toss cooked chicken cubes in plain yogurt with a pinch of finely chopped fresh mint to make a refreshing Greek-style pita.

Mix up chopped raw mushrooms, eggplant and feta cheese for a vegetarian bite.

Pita pizza

This is a fun lunch that is quick to prepare. You can improvise and add your favorite toppings.

Serves 2   Prep. time: 5 mins   Cooking time: 8—10 mins

2	**pita breads**
1/2 cup/125 ml	**tomato sauce**
2 oz/60 g	**thinly sliced salami**
1/2 cup/125 ml	**grated Cheddar cheese**

At camp:

Put the pita in a large skillet and cover it with the tomato sauce. Move the pitas occasionally to prevent them sticking or burning.
Layer with slices of salami. Sprinkle on the grated cheese. Heat gently until the cheese is melted and you have a freshly made pita pizza.

Tomato, cucumber and red onion salad

A really easy salad to make, but do plan ahead here because it needs about an hour for all the ingredients to blend. However, it is worth that wait.

Serves **6**   Prep. time: **10** mins   Standing time: **1** hour

2	**cucumbers**
1/3 cup/75 ml	**red wine vinegar**
1 tbsp/15 ml	**sugar**
1 tsp/5 ml	**salt**
✱ **3**	**large tomatoes, de-seeded and chopped (not too finely)**
✱ **1**	**small red onion, chopped**
small bunch	**fresh mint, chopped**
3 tbsp/45 ml	**oil**
	salt and pepper, to taste

At camp:

Peel the cucumbers and slice them in half lengthwise, de-seed and slice across. In a large bowl, mix together the cucumber, vinegar, sugar and salt. Leave to stand for about 1 hour, during which time you can chop the remaining ingredients. When you are ready to serve, add the tomatoes, onion, mint and oil, and toss. Season with salt and pepper to taste.

Trailside tips:

- Save fuel by undercooking foods slightly and letting them sit for a few moments, covered, to finish cooking. This works especially well with rice and vegetables.

- If your trip is over several weeks and you plan to visit some towns, pack non-perishable provisions that can be mailed to yourself at a point on your itinerary, and top up your supplies.

- It's always a nice idea to pack a "surprise" to pull out of the pack when your party least expects it, and perhaps most needs it. Licorice, raisins and peanuts, candy — high energy, high morale!

On the go apple 'n' nut snack

This is a clever way of packing the calories in while on the move and has been a boy scout staple for decades.

Serves **2**   Prep. time: **3** mins

2 tbsp/30 ml	**peanut butter**
2 tbsp/30 ml	**peanuts**
2 tbsp/30 ml	**raisins and/or chocolate chips**
2	**large apples**

At camp:

Mix the peanut butter, peanuts, raisins and/or chocolate chips into a sticky paste. Core the apples and stuff the holes with the paste. If there is any left over, enjoy as a perk for the cook. Wrap each apple in plastic wrap or in a plastic bag with as much air squeezed out as possible. Keep in your pocket or backpack until you feel like a bite.

Black bean spread

Dips and spreads are made for eating on the trail along with bread or crackers, and robust flavors are what you need when eating outdoors. This spread is very tasty and nutritious and can be prepared ahead.

Serves 6 (over 2 lunches)   Prep. time: 5 mins

14-oz/400-g	**can black beans**
2	**cloves garlic, minced**
4 tbsp/60 ml	**hot or medium salsa (according to taste)**
1/2 cup/125 ml	**cottage cheese**
1 tsp/5 ml	**hot pepper sauce, optional**
2 tsp/10 ml	**ground cumin**
1 tsp/5 ml	**chopped fresh coriander**
	salt and pepper, to taste

At home:

Drain the beans of their liquid and place them in a blender with all the other ingredients. Blend until smooth.

Pack in two airtight containers; each one should provide enough dip for six people. Refrigerate until required. On the trail, eat it on the first day unless you can keep it in a cooler.

Or at camp:

Drain the beans and place in bowl with all the other ingredients.

Use a fork, first to crush all ingredients and then to mix them into as smooth a paste as possible.

Bacon and Cheddar spread

Tasty and crunchy, this spread is sublime on hot bread in the great outdoors.

Serves **8**   Prep. time: **15** mins   Cooking time: **5** mins

10	**slices bacon**
2 cups/500 ml	**grated Cheddar cheese**
1 tbsp/15 ml	**grated red onion**
1 cup/250 ml	**creamy salad dressing (bought or homemade — see recipe below)**

At camp:
Fry the bacon in a skillet over a medium heat until well cooked and crispy.
Drain and crumble into pieces.
In a bowl, mix the bacon, cheese, onion and dressing thoroughly. Serve on bread or crackers. If you are able, it is good chilled for an hour before serving.

Instant creamy salad dressing

1/2	**clove garlic, minced**
1 tbsp/15 ml	**oil**
1/2 cup/125 ml	**sour cream**
1/4 cup/50 ml	**milk**

At camp:
Soften the garlic in a pan with the oil over a low heat for about 1 minute.
Add the sour cream and milk. Stir frequently until the mixture thickens. Do not let it boil. Use immediately.

Pasta bowl

This is fast food for a filling lunch. On a cold day, it is great to stop for a hot lunch and this one warms you down to your socks.

Serves **4**   Prep. time: **5** mins   Cooking time: **20** mins

1 cup/250 ml	**dried pasta (such as conchiole or macaroni)**
1	**green bell pepper, chopped**
1	**large tomato, finely chopped**
1	**onion, finely chopped**
14-oz/400-g	**can kidney beans**
2 cups/500 ml	**chicken broth**
8-oz/235-g	**can chickpeas**
1 tsp/5 ml	**Worcestershire sauce**
1 tsp/5 ml	**dried basil**
1	**garlic clove, finely chopped**

At home:
Save time by mixing together all the dry ingredients in one bag, and repacking the canned beans in plastic bags.

At camp:
Mix together all the ingredients in a large pan, cover and bring to a boil.
Simmer for 15 minutes, stirring occasionally, until the pasta is *al dente*. You can add an extra 1/2 cup/125 ml pasta if you want to thicken the dish up.

Speedy pasta

If you need an energy-packed meal but don't have too much time, put on a pan of water to boil, and make this speedy hi-carb dish. It can be prepared in about 15 minutes and tastes great.

Serves **2**   Prep. time: **15** minutes   Cooking time: **10** mins

1/2 tsp/2 ml	salt
1 cup/250 ml	pasta (such as penne or rigatoni)
1 tbsp/15 ml	oil
2	tomatoes, chopped
1 cup/250 ml	grated Parmesan
2 tsp/10 ml	dried basil
1 tsp/5 ml	dried parsley

At camp:

Bring a large pot of salted water to a boil, add the pasta and cook on a gentle rolling boil for 7 minutes. When *al dente*, remove from the heat and drain.
Add the oil, tomatoes, cheese, and herbs. Toss everything together to coat the pasta and serve immediately. Grate or sprinkle over some extra Parmesan.

No-pot stew

A simple but filling stew cooked in the bag so that no pots need to be washed up afterward. It's a versatile dish because you can add almost anything to it.

Serves **4**   Prep. time: **5** mins   Cooking time: **30** mins

✦	2	**large onions, sliced**
✦	1	**large green pepper, sliced**
✦	2	**large carrots, chopped into small chunks**
✦	2	**medium potatoes, peeled and chopped into small chunks**
✦		**chopped sausage, leftover diced chicken, etc.**
	2	**cloves garlic, minced**
	1 tbsp/15 ml	**butter**
		salt and pepper, to taste

At camp:

Place the vegetables and meat on a sheet of foil, smear with minced garlic and butter, and salt and pepper to taste. Sprinkle with a little water, then fold the foil into a packet. Suspend above the campfire flames (not in direct contact) for about 30 minutes. If using uncooked meat, ensure it is fully cooked. Serve with rice or noodles.

Apple and turkey stirfry

The great advantage of stirfry is that you can prepare a quick, light meal that is full of flavor and is healthy and nutritious. If you do a little preparation after breakfast, you can rustle up this lunch in less than 15 minutes.

Serves **6**   Prep. time: **5** mins (standing time 30 mins)   Cooking time: **7–9** mins

1/2 tsp/2 ml	ground black pepper
2	cloves garlic, crushed
1 tbsp/15 ml	brown sugar
2 tbsp/30 ml	soy sauce
1 tbsp/15 ml	Worcestershire sauce
1 tbsp/15 ml	cornstarch
1/2 cup/125 ml	unsweetened apple juice
1 1/2 lbs/680 g	turkey breast, diced
1 tbsp/15 ml	oil
1 cup/250 ml	snow peas
4	carrots, finely chopped

At camp:

Mix together the pepper, garlic, sugar, soy sauce, Worcestershire sauce, cornstarch and apple juice in a large, plastic, sealable bag. Add the diced turkey. You can do this in camp before heading out for the day.

When you stop for lunch, heat the oil in a pan over a high heat. Add the turkey mixture and stirfry for 5 to 6 minutes. As the turkey cooks, push it to the sides of the pan and add the vegetables in the center and cook for a further 3 minutes.

Serve the turkey and vegetables alone or with rice.

Fruit log

Because this finger food has a high sugar content, it will keep well for several days if you make it in advance. However, it is quick and simple enough to throw together in a few moments in the camp kitchen.

Makes **10** slices   Prep. time: **15** mins

1/2 cup/125 ml	**chopped dates**
1/2 cup/125 ml	**chopped raisins**
1/2 cup/125 ml	**shredded coconut**
1/2 cup/125 ml	**chopped mixed nuts**
1/2 cup/125 ml	**glacé cherries, chopped**
1/2 cup/125 ml	**chopped dried apricots**
1/2 cup/125 ml	**peaches, chopped (fresh or canned)**
1/4 cup/50 ml	**chopped dried figs**
2 tbsp/30 ml	**orange juice**
1 tbsp/15 ml	**confectioner's sugar**

At home:

Make sure that all the fruits and nuts are chopped as finely as possible and mix them all together in a large bowl. Stir in the orange juice and then with your hands, thoroughly bind this mixture together. Lift the mixture out onto a board and form it into the shape of a log about 8–10 in/20–25 cm long and 4 in/10 cm in diameter. Sprinkle with the sugar.

(An alternative is to omit the mixed nuts from the mixture and instead roll the finished log over the nuts to coat.)

Pack the log in an airtight plastic bag or slice into portions and wrap individually. Refrigerate until needed, but if packed in airtight bags this log will keep for many days on the trail — assuming you can resist the temptation to eat it sooner!

Peanut crisp

Peanuts are packed with energy and by the time you have added the honey, sugar and fruit, you will have no trouble striding out all afternoon.

Serves **6**   Prep. time: **10** mins   Cooking time: **10** mins

1 tbsp/15 ml	**margarine**
1/4 cup/50 ml	**brown sugar**
2 tbsp/30 ml	**honey**
1/2 cup/125 ml	**crunchy peanut butter**
11/4 cups/300 ml	**cereal flakes**
3 tbsp/45 ml	**assorted mixed dried fruits**

At camp:
Grease an 18 x 26-in/46 x 66-cm baking tray with margarine.

Place the sugar and honey in a medium-size pan and stir over medium heat until the sugar is dissolved. Watch it continuously to ensure it does not burn. Remove from the heat and stir in the peanut butter, combining until the mixture is smooth. Add the cereal flakes and dried fruits.

Spread the mixture over the baking tray about 1 in/2.5 cm deep. When cool, cut the peanut crisp into squares to serve, or seal in plastic wrap for individual packing.

One-pot suppers & sides

Nutritionally, dinner is the most important meal of the day after breakfast. When trekking, you are usually tired, footsore and certainly hungry by dinnertime, and it's often difficult to muster up the energy to prepare a decent meal. However, it is a good idea to refuel your body overnight to keep warm and rehydrated. The following recipes are devised not only to be nutritious, they are all temptingly quick to make. One-pot suppers are made with the minimum of fuss and adding a variety of sides will turn your camp meal into a "psychological" banquet.

Lentil chili

This is a great tasting and nutritious vegetable chili. Bulgur wheat has all the nutrients of whole wheat, but adds bulk and doesn't need to be cooked for so long.

Serves **6**   Prep. time: **10** mins   Cooking time: **35** mins

2 tbsp/30 ml	oil
❋ 1	large onion, finely chopped
❋ 1	green bell pepper, chopped
4	cloves garlic, minced
1 cup/250 ml	dried lentils
1 cup/250 ml	bulgur wheat
❋ 3	large potatoes, peeled and cut into small cubes
3 cups/750 ml	vegetable stock
14-oz/400-g	can chopped tomatoes
2 tsp/10 ml	chili powder
1 tbsp/15 ml	ground cumin

At camp:

Heat the oil in a large pot over a medium heat. Add the onion, bell pepper and garlic and sauté for 5 minutes until softened. Stir in the remaining ingredients.
Bring the mixture to a boil, cover and simmer gently for 30 minutes, stirring occasionally, until the lentils are tender. Serve immediately while piping hot in bowls.

Chicken and apple stew

This makes a very nutritious stew and you can add additional favorite vegetables if you wish. Ideally, it is made in a Dutch oven, but you can make it in a pan on a camping stove as long as you have plenty of fuel.

Serves 4   Prep. time: 10 mins   Cooking time: 45 mins

1 tbsp/15 ml	oil
1 lb/450 g	skinless chicken breast, cut into cubes
pinch	nutmeg
1 tbsp/15 ml	Dijon mustard
	salt and pepper, to taste
2 cups/500 ml	chicken stock (or use 3 chicken stock cubes dissolved in water)
1/4 cup/50 ml	apple cider vinegar
4	cloves
1	large potato, peeled and cut into small pieces
2	carrots, finely sliced
4	red apples, peeled, cored and cut into thick slices
1 cup/250 ml	unsweetened applesauce

At camp:

Heat the oil in a large pan over medium heat. Add the chicken and cook for about 5 minutes, turning frequently, until golden brown. Add the nutmeg, salt and pepper, and the mustard. Stir to ensure the chicken is well coated. Add the stock, vinegar, cloves, potatoes and carrots.

Bring to a boil, cover and simmer gently for about 15 minutes.

Add the apples and cook for a further 15 minutes. Avoid overcooking the apples because you want them to retain shape and texture. Remove the meat and vegetables and keep them warm in a pot by the fire.

Add the applesauce to the liquid mixture and boil for a further 5 minutes. Serve the chicken and vegetables in bowls, with the hot broth poured over.

Pasta Alfredo

Alfredo sauce combines the richness of cream with the tanginess of Parmesan cheese — ingredients that go wonderfully well with pasta. This is a delicious meal that can be rustled up while the rest of the gang put the tents up and light the fire.

Serves **8**   Prep. time: **10** mins   Cooking time: **10** mins

1 lb/450 g	pasta (such as penne or rigatoni)
4 tbsp/60 ml	butter or margarine
2 cups/500 ml	sliced mushrooms
1/2 cup/125 ml	heavy cream
1 cup/250 ml	cooked ham, cut into thin strips
2 lbs/900 g	skinless, boneless chicken breasts, cut into cubes
2/3 cup/150 ml	grated Parmesan
	pepper, to taste

At camp:

In a large pot, bring salted water to a boil and cook the pasta for 10 minutes, until it is *al dente*.

In a skillet melt half of the butter over medium heat and sauté the mushrooms until brown. Add the cream to the mushrooms and, stirring frequently, add the ham and chicken and heat through.

When the pasta is ready, remove it from the heat, drain, return to the pot and toss with the remaining butter and the mushroom mixture, stirring it around thoroughly to distribute the ingredients. Serve in large bowls with a sprinkling of Parmesan and lots of black pepper.

Dutch-oven lasagne

A delicious and easy-to-make camp "lasagne." It takes quite a long time to cook so is best made in a Dutch oven over the hot embers of a campfire. This is not a meal for the lightweight camper but, if you are in a large group sharing the load or with a vehicle, it is well worth the effort.

Serves **8** to **12**   Prep. time: **15** mins   Cooking time: **45** mins

✺ 2 lbs/900 g	ground beef
	tomato and basil sauce (see below)
2 cups/500 ml	ricotta or cottage cheese
3	eggs or egg powder equivalent
1 tsp/5 ml	dried oregano
1/2 tsp/2 ml	dried basil
12	sheets oven-ready lasagne pasta
4 cups/1,000 ml	grated Cheddar cheese
1/4 cup/50 ml	grated Parmesan

Tomato and basil sauce:

✺ 10	tomatoes
1/2 cup/125 ml	fresh basil, finely chopped
1/2 cup/125 ml	olive oil
4	cloves garlic, chopped
	salt and black pepper, to taste

At home:

To make the tomato and basil sauce: De-seed and finely dice the tomatoes. Place in a large bowl, add the basil, oil, garlic, and salt and pepper. Mix thoroughly and let stand for 1 hour before packing in an airtight container. Refrigerate. Use within a day or two.

At camp:

Set a Dutch oven over the embers of the fire and preheat. Add the meat straight into the oven and seal in its juices until brown, about 5 to 6 minutes. Remove from the heat and set the meat aside in a bowl.

Add the tomato and basil sauce to the meat and mix thoroughly. In a separate bowl, mix together the ricotta cheese, eggs and herbs. Now line the base and sides of the oven with foil brushed with melted butter and return to the fire. Make sure the foil extends well up the sides of the oven to enable lifting out of the cooked lasagne.

To assemble the lasagne:
Spread a layer of meat sauce evenly over the foil in the base of the oven. Cover with three sheets of lasagna. The pasta will expand during cooking, so the pieces need not overlap each other.

Spread a layer of ricotta cheese mixture on top of the lasagne sheets. Then layer another portion of meat sauce and a layer of Cheddar cheese. Add more layers of lasagne, ricotta, meat sauce and Cheddar until all except 1 cup/250 ml Cheddar is used up. Sprinkle Parmesan over the top. Cover the lasagne with foil.

Cover with the lid and rake up some hot embers over the top of the oven. Bake for about 30 minutes.

Remove the lid and foil and sprinkle the remaining Cheddar on top of the lasagne and bake for a further 10 minutes. Remove the oven from the fire, allow to stand for about 5 minutes and lift out the lasagne. Let it stand for a few minutes after which it is easier to cut into portions. Serve hot.

Meat loaf

This recipe is good for four hungry people. If there is any left over, eat it cold on the trail the next day. It is not a conventional meat loaf recipe as it contains carrot which adds a subtle taste sensation. You can prepare and cook it at home, or on the trail you can use a Dutch oven, a loaf pan, or fashion a foil container. The only preparation needed is chopping the vegetables and mixing the ingredients to form the loaf.

Serves **4**   Prep. time **5** mins   Cooking time: about **1** hour

✸	**1 lb/450 g**	**ground beef**
✸	**2**	**large carrots, shredded**
✸	**1**	**large onion, chopped**
✸	**1**	**green bell pepper, diced, optional**
	1 cup/250 ml	**rolled oats**
	1	**egg or egg powder equivalent**
	1 cup/250 ml	**milk**
	1 tsp/5 ml	**Worcestershire sauce**
		salt and pepper, to taste

At home:
Preheat the oven to 350°F/180°C. Mix all the ingredients in a large bowl until well blended. Place in a greased 9 x 5 x 3-in/23 x 13 x 8-cm loaf pan and cook for 1 hour. The loaf should be firm on the outside and moist on the inside and the meat thoroughly cooked. Remove from heat, pour off any fat and allow to cool completely. Wrap in plastic and then foil and refrigerate until needed.

Or at camp:
Preheat a Dutch oven and place a sheet of greased foil on the bottom. Prepare the vegetables and place all ingredients in a large bowl, mix thoroughly and form into a loaf shape. Place the loaf on the foil and cook for 1 hour. Remove, allow to cool, and carve.
Serve sliced with your choice of side dishes.

Lemon couscous with chicken

This is a very quick and easy meal to prepare because the couscous cooks faster and bulks up better than rice. The lemon adds a refreshing zing.

Serves **2**   Prep. time: **5** mins   Cooking time: **15–20** mins

4	**chicken bouillon cubes**
2 lbs/900 g	**chicken chunks**
pinch	**lemon zest**
1 cup/125 ml	**couscous**
1 tbsp/15 ml	**oil**
1 tsp/5 ml	**dried oregano**
1 tsp/5 ml	**dried parsley**
	salt and pepper, to taste

At home:
To dehydrate the chicken, dice 2 lbs/900 g skinned chicken breasts to produce 8 oz/225 g of dehydrated product (see p. 19). Pack in an airtight bag.

At camp:
To rehydrate the chicken, add 2 cups/500 ml water and leave it to reconstitute in a sealed plastic bag. If you plan to eat the chicken for dinner, add the water earlier in the day (at the lunch stop).

Fill a large pan with 3 cups/750 ml water and bring to a boil. Add the bouillon cubes, diced chicken and lemon zest and stir. Add the couscous and then immediately remove from the heat. Let the pan stand covered for about 5 minutes.

Fluff up the couscous with a fork and at the same time stir in the oil, oregano and parsley, and season to taste. Serve hot.

Fish in foil

This is a fast and delicious way to prepare fish whether you have caught it yourself or bought it locally. The recipe works for almost any kind of fish but is particularly good with mahi-mahi and tilapia. You can prepare it in a Dutch oven or on the grill.

Serves **4**   Prep. time: **10** mins   Cooking time: **10–15** mins

2	**fresh fish (cleaned to produce 4 fillets)**
2	**fresh jalapeno peppers**
2 tbsp/30 ml	**oil**
1 tsp/5 ml	**salt**
2	**cloves garlic, minced**
2 tsp/10 ml	**black pepper**
2	**lemons, cut into 8 segments**

At camp:

Preheat the Dutch oven or grill. Place each fillet on its own square of aluminum foil. Prepare the jalapenos by cutting off the top and, using a thin-bladed knife, dislodge and discard the seeds (the seeds are intensely hot). Slice the peppers thinly. Don't touch your eyes while working with peppers and wash your hands as soon as you have finished.

Brush the fillets with oil, season with salt, garlic and pepper. Arrange the jalapeno slices and squeeze the juice of 2 segments of the lemon on top of each fillet. Fold the foil into a package, ensuring the sides are sealed. Bake in the oven or over the grill for 10 to 15 minutes (large fillets will take 5 to 10 minutes longer to cook). The fish is cooked when it flakes away easily with a fork. Serve hot.

Ginger beef

You can enjoy a taste of the East with this grilled dish. Hoisin sauce is made from fermented soy beans, sugar, garlic and vinegar and is both sweet and spicy, and delicious basted onto barbecue ribs, chicken or, in this case, beef. It is available from Asian stores.

Serves 6   Prep. time: 25 mins   Cooking time: 15 mins

1/2 cup/125 ml	**hoisin sauce**
1/2 cup/125 ml	**sherry**
1/2 cup/125 ml	**soy sauce**
4	**scallions, finely chopped**
4	**cloves garlic, minced**
2 tbsp/30 ml	**ground ginger**
6 x 8-oz/225-g	**steaks (or 3 lbs/1.3 kg flank steak or equivalent)**

At camp:

Mix the hoisin sauce, sherry, soy sauce, scallions, garlic and ginger together in a large, sealable plastic bag.

Cut the steaks across the grain into thick slices, about 2 in/5 cm thick.

Put the steak into the bag with the sauce, shake well and allow to marinate for up to 4 hours.

Fire up the grill, push the steak onto skewers and cook to your liking, about 2 minutes each side for medium rare, 3 minutes each side for medium to well done.

Hungry hiker parcels

Serves 4 hungry hikers   Prep. time: 10 mins   Cooking time: 30 mins

✿	1 lb/450 g	**ground beef**
✿	1	**large potato, peeled and cut into small cubes**
✿	1	**large carrot, peeled and cut into small strips**
✿	1	**large onion, finely chopped**
	4 tbsp/60 ml	**ketchup or tomato paste**
		salt and pepper, to taste

At camp:

Divide the meat into four portions and shape into patties. Mix and divide the prepared vegetables into four portions.

For each patty, take a square of foil and spread 1 tbsp/15 ml of ketchup or tomato paste, mixed with a little water, in the center. Place a meat patty on top of the ketchup, and then one portion of the mixed vegetables on top of the patty. Season to taste.

Fold the foil to form four parcels, sealing their tops and sides. Cook in hot embers for about 30 minutes. Serve piping hot.

Sausage risotto

This version of risotto is the perfect one-pot meal. It has to take 30 minutes of your attention, so if you are starving it's not the best choice, unless you can provide some nibbles to eat while the dish is cooking. It is good with chicken or even fish flakes instead of the sausage — and even tastes good without any meat at all.

Serves 6   Prep. time: 10 mins   Cooking time: 20–30 mins

1 tbsp/15 ml	oil
2	cloves garlic, minced
1	large onion, finely chopped
3 cups/750 ml	long grain rice
4 cups/1 l	hot chicken stock
1 cup/250 ml	canned chopped tomatoes, drained
1/2 cup/125 ml	sliced mushrooms
2	large Italian salami sausage
	(about 4 oz/110 g each), casings removed and sliced
1 tbsp/15 ml	dried parsley

At camp:

Heat the oil in a pan over medium heat and add the minced garlic and onion. Sauté until golden. Add the rice and stir it around to coat the grains.

Add 3 cups/750 ml of the hot chicken stock and allow the liquid to simmer until the rice is soft to bite and is fluffy (about 15 to 20 minutes). Add spoonfuls of the remaining stock, stirring occasionally, until absorbed by the rice.

Add the tomatoes, mushrooms and sausage and simmer until all the ingredients are hot. Just before removing from the heat, mix in the parsley.

Ham and cheese potato stew

This is a great recipe for when you want something hot, filling and you want it fast. You can rustle up this dish in a Dutch oven, in a pan on the camp stove or you can prepare it in advance at home.

Serves 4   Prep. time: 5 mins   Cooking time: 20 mins

2 tbsp/30 ml	margarine
1	small onion, finely chopped
1¹/2 tbsp/22 ml	all-purpose flour
1 cup/250 ml	milk, or reconstituted powdered milk
	salt and pepper, to taste
1 cup/250 ml	diced cooked ham
2	medium potatoes, thinly sliced
1/2 cup/125 ml	grated Cheddar cheese
1 tbsp/15 ml	bread crumbs

At home:

Preheat the oven to 400°F/200°C. Melt the margarine in a small pan and sauté the onion for about 1 minute. Slowly add the flour, stirring continuously, to form a paste. Gradually add the milk until the sauce thickens. Season to taste.

Place the ham and potatoes in a casserole dish and add the sauce.

Cook for 15 minutes, remove, sprinkle the cheese and bread crumbs over the top and cook for a further 5 minutes. Remove and allow to cool. Pack in an airtight bag. Refrigerate until you are leaving and use within two days.

Or at camp:

Line a Dutch oven with foil or grease a large cooking pot and layer with the ham and potato.

Make the sauce as above and pour it over the layers of ham and potato.

Cook over a medium heat for 15 to 20 minutes. Sprinkle the bread crumbs and grated cheese over the top and cook for a few more minutes until the cheese has melted. Ladle out to serve.

Curry couscous

Couscous is the camper's friend because it cooks faster than rice, bulks up better and imparts an interesting texture and flavor.

Serves **4**   Prep. time: **5** mins   Cooking time: **10** mins

1 cup/250 ml	**mixed vegetables (such as peas, carrots and beans)**
1 tsp/5 ml	**curry powder**
1	**beef stock cube**
1 tbsp/15 ml	**oil**
1 cup/250 ml	**couscous**

At home:
Dehydrate the vegetables (see p. 19).

At camp:
Fill a medium-size pan with 1¹/₂ cups/325 ml water. Add the vegetables, curry powder, crumbled beef stock cube and oil and bring to a boil.

Once the mixture has reached a boil, add the couscous and mix well. Immediately remove from the heat, cover and stand for 5 to 10 minutes until the couscous has softened. Serve hot.

Corn fritters

You can prepare all the dry ingredients for this dish at home and pack them in one bag for convenience. These fritters are great with the Chicken and apple stew (p. 95) and Meat loaf (p. 100).

Serves 4   Prep. time: 7 mins   Cooking time: 4–5 mins

1/2 cup/125 ml	milk or reconstituted powdered milk
1 tbsp/15 ml	egg powder
1/2 tsp/2 ml	salt
1 1/2 tsp/7 ml	baking powder
1 cup/250 ml	all-purpose flour
1 cup/250 ml	dried or freeze-dried corn
1 tbsp/15 ml	oil

At home:

Combine all the ingredients except the corn and oil, mix thoroughly and pack in one sealable plastic bag or container.

At camp:

Soak the corn in 2 cups/500 ml warm water for 5 minutes, then drain.
Add the corn to the dry ingredients and blend well. Add a little more water, one teaspoon at a time, until the mixture forms a thick paste.
Heat the oil in a skillet over a hot flame and drop heaped tablespoons of fritter mix onto the pan. Reduce the heat to medium and cook for 2 to 3 minutes until the bottom of the fritter is brown. Flip and cook the other side for 1 to 2 minutes. Serve immediately.

Mexican rice

The diverse ingredients make this an out-of-the-ordinary side dish. You can also double the ingredients and prepare it as a main dinner dish. Eat with Lentil chili (p. 94), Fish in foil (p. 102) or Meat loaf (p. 100).

Serves: **2**   Prep. time: **10** mins   Cooking time: **10** mins

	1 cup/250 ml	**rice**
✺	**1/2 cup/125 ml**	**corn**
✺	**1 tbsp/15 ml**	**sliced onions**
	1 tbsp/15 ml	**sliced black olives**
✺	**1/4 cup/50 ml**	**chopped tomatoes**
✺	**1/4 cup/50 ml**	**diced bell pepper**
	2 tbsp/30 ml	**chili powder**
		salt and pepper, to taste
		grated cheese, optional

At home:
When dehydrating vegetables at home, do large batches at a time and take what you need for each recipe's requirements. For this recipe you can pack all the dried vegetables together in an airtight bag.

At camp:
In a pan, boil 1 cup/250 ml salted water and add the rice. Cover and simmer for 15 minutes until all the liquid is absorbed and the rice is soft and fluffy. Set aside to keep warm.

In another pan, boil 1 cup/250 ml water and add the corn, onions, olives, tomatoes and peppers. Add the chili powder to the vegetables and season to taste. The mixture should be moist but not runny.

Stir the rice into the vegetable mixture and serve hot.

If you wish to use this recipe as a base for a one-pot rice dish and add pieces of beef or turkey, or beans, simply allow the additions to heat through.

Sprinkle a little grated cheese on top before serving.

Scalloped potatoes

This is a convenient way to have potatoes available for any meal on the trail because you can pack everything you need in one bag to make this delicious side dish.

Each bag serves **4**   Prep. time: **10** mins plus dehydrating
Cooking time: **20** mins at home, **20** mins at the campsite

4 lbs/1.8 kg	**potatoes**
2 cups/500 ml	**powdered milk**
1 cup/250 ml	**grated Parmesan**
2	**onions, sliced**
¹/₂ cup/125 ml	**bacon bits**
¹/₂ cup/125 ml	**all-purpose flour**
¹/₂ cup/125 ml	**coffee creamer powder**
	salt and pepper, to taste

At home:

Peel the potatoes and boil them for 20 minutes. Drain and allow to cool.
Cut the potatoes into ¹/₄-in/6-mm thick slices, place on a large baking tray and dehydrate in the oven at about 130°F/56°C for 5 to 6 hours.
When dried, divide into four separate bags and add to each bag: a quarter of the powdered milk, Parmesan, onion slices, bacon bits, flour and creamer. Season to taste. Seal.

At camp:

To rehydrate the bags, add enough water to cover the contents and let stand to for 1 hour.
When reconstituted, place the contents of the bags in a pan and bring to a boil. Cover and simmer until the potatoes thicken up. Remove from the heat and allow to stand for 5 to 10 minutes. Fluff up with a fork and serve hot.

Potatoes and green beans

While you can dehydrate all the vegetables for this side dish before you set off, then rehydrate for 30 to 45 minutes, fresh ingredients are recommended. Either way, it is a simple and nourishing vegetable combination.

Serves **4**   Prep. time: **5** mins   Cooking time: **5–10** mins

✺ **3**	**medium potatoes, boiled and sliced**
✺ **1/2 cup/125 ml**	**cooked green beans, or 8 oz/250 g fresh green beans**
✺ **1**	**onion, sliced**
4-oz/110-g	**packet instant onion soup mix**

At camp:

Place the vegetables in the center of a piece of foil and sprinkle over the onion soup mix. Fold the foil into a sealed parcel and place close to the fire or stove until all the ingredients are heated and cooked through.

Carrot and cabbage salad

This is an unusual combination for a salad but it works well, especially as a side dish with the Sausage risotto (p. 105), or for lunch.

Serves 4   Prep. time: 5 mins

⚙	½ cup/125 ml	shredded cabbage
⚙	½ cup/125 ml	shredded carrot
	pinch	celery salt
	¼ cup/50 ml	raisins
	1 tbsp/15 ml	oil
	1 tbsp/15 ml	red wine vinegar

At home:

Shred the cabbage and carrot and dehydrate in the oven (see page 19).
To produce ½ cup/125 ml you will need to use at least 1 lb/450 g of fresh produce.
Store in airtight bags.

At camp:

Rehydrate the cabbage and carrot in 1½ cups/375 ml water for 20 to 25 minutes.
Drain and add the celery salt.
Stir in the raisins, oil and vinegar and mix well. Serve cold.

Camp coleslaw

This is a quick and refreshing side dish whether it's hot or cold. You can use dehydrated cabbage and onion and combine them at home to save time.

Serves **4** to **6**   Prep. time: **10** mins

1	**medium-size cabbage, shredded finely**
1/2	**cucumber, peeled and finely chopped**
1	**medium onion, sliced**
1 tbsp/15 ml	**raisins, optional (but worth it)**
	salt and pepper, to taste
1 cup/250 ml	**mayonnaise**
1/4 cup/50 ml	**unsweetened orange juice**

At home:

Finely shred the cabbage, spread on a large baking tray and dehydrate in the oven at around 130°F/55°C for 5 to 6 hours.

At camp:

Reconstitute the cabbage by placing in a bowl and covering with water. Add additional water as necessary until the cabbage is fully reconstituted, then drain.
Mix the cabbage, cucumber, onion, raisins, and salt and pepper together in a bowl.
Blend the mayonnaise and orange juice together and pour it over the cabbage mixture.
Toss thoroughly to coat the vegetables. Serve cold.

Breads
& biscuits

Bread is one the great camping foods because it is so versatile. It complements any meal. Crispy bread and rye bread will last for several days. When it is getting stale, you can break it up and add it to stews and other dishes. Many of the bread recipes that follow can be made either at home or at camp — so enjoy!

Trail bread

Just the smell of cooking bread on the trail makes the effort worthwhile. This recipe was developed by American settlers as they moved west on the wagon trains. It couldn't be easier now with the use of a Dutch oven. If you prefer to make it ahead at home, it freezes well too. On the trail it will keep for three or four days and longer in cool weather. It is a versatile recipe: use more honey by reducing the equivalent amount of water or sprinkle in golden raisins or add thinly sliced jerky.

Makes **2** loaves (30–36 slices)   Prep. time: **5** mins   Cooking time: **45** mins

1/3 cup/75 ml	honey
2 1/2 tbsp/37 ml	active dry yeast
3 cups/750 ml	warm water
2 tbsp/30 ml	vegetable oil
2 tbsp/30 ml	salt
9 cups/2.25 l	bread flour

At camp:

In a large bowl, dissolve the honey and yeast in the warm water and let stand for about 10 minutes.

Stir in the oil, salt and 4 cups/950 ml of the flour. Gradually blend in the remaining flour until you have a firm dough. Remove from the bowl and, on a lightly floured baking mat, knead for 10 to 15 minutes until soft. The dough should not stick to your hands. Place in a lightly oiled bowl, cover and allow to rise for about 1 hour. The dough needs to be warm so stand it near the fire or stove if the air is cool.

Divide the dough into two equal pieces and shape into loaves. Place in two lightly greased 9 x 5 x 3-in/23 x 13 x 8-cm loaf pans. Cover the pans with a damp cloth and allow them to rise for another 35 to 40 minutes until they have doubled in volume. While this is happening, preheat a Dutch oven to a medium-hot temperature.

Bake the loaves for 45 to 60 minutes.

The loaves are ready when they give a hollow sound when tapped on the bottom. (If you bake this at home the oven temperature should be 375°F /190°C.)

Serve warm with lots of butter or honey.

Damper bread

This is a traditional Australian bread that can be cooked in a Dutch oven, but is best baked on the hot coals of a campfire.

Makes **1** large loaf   Prep. time: **10** mins   Cooking time: **30** mins

4 cups/1,000 ml   all-purpose flour
1/2 tsp/2 ml   salt
2 tbsp/30 ml   butter
11/2 cups/375 ml milk or reconstituted powdered milk

At camp:

Mix the flour and salt in a large bowl. Rub in the butter with your hands until you have a bread crumb-like texture. Make a well in the center and slowly pour in the milk, stirring to combine until you have a firm dough.
Place the dough on to a floured baking mat and knead into a round shape.
Place on a greased baking sheet or sheet of foil and, using a knife, make a criss-cross in the top the dough. Bake in a Dutch oven sitting in hot ashes of a campfire for about 30 minutes, until golden brown. Alternatively, place the dough on a griddle directly on top of the hot embers. Serve warm with butter and honey.

Bannock

Bannock bread originated in Scotland and Ireland centuries ago. Emigrants have carried the recipe around the world and adapted it. Traditionally it is a flat, unleavened bread made of oatmeal or barley flour and is usually cooked on a griddle or on hot stones. Fresh blueberries make an excellent addition to this bread. Because it is easy to make and uses so few ingredients it has long been a favorite with travelers and variations of it are found worldwide.

Makes 1 x 1 lb/450 g cake   Prep. time: **10** mins
Cooking time: **10–15** mins

4 cups/1,000 ml	**all-purpose or potato flour**
2¹/₂ tbsp/37 ml	**baking powder**
1 tsp/5 ml	**salt**
1 tsp/5 ml	**sugar**
	dab of butter

At camp:

Mix the flour, baking powder, salt and sugar thoroughly. Gradually stir in enough water to make a thick, smooth batter, about the consistency of light cream.
Heat a dab of butter in a large skillet and pour in enough batter to a depth of about 1 in/2.5 cm. Place the skillet on hot coals.
Cook for 5 to 7 minutes and then flip the bread over to cook the other side for 5 to 7 minutes, until golden brown. Check the bannock is cooked all the way through by poking a skewer in the center. If no dough sticks it is cooked.
To serve, tear the bannock apart rather than cutting it with a knife, and spread with honey or butter and devour.

Indian fry bread

Also known as Navajo taco, this bread has been made by Native Americans for centuries. It's enjoyed with savory or sweet fillings or rolled in sugar for a dessert.

Makes **24** rounds   Prep. time: **25** mins   Cooking time: **2–3** mins each

2 cups/500 ml	**all-purpose flour**
2 tsp/10 ml	**baking powder**
1/4 cup/50 ml	**sugar, optional**
1/2 cup/125 ml	**powdered milk**
pinch	**salt**
1 cup/250 ml	**warm water**
	vegetable oil, for deep-frying

At camp:

Mix the flour, baking powder, sugar, powdered milk and salt together in a large bowl. Stir in the warm water and mix with a fork and your hands to produce a soft dough. Let stand for 30 minutes to rise.

Pull off pieces of the dough and fashion into rounds about golf-ball size, 1/4 in/6 mm in diameter and flatten.

Add oil to a skillet to a depth of 1 in/2.5 cm and heat to 350°F/180°C. Test whether it is the right temperature by dropping a piece of dough into the oil — if it sizzles immediately, the oil is hot enough. Deep-fry 3 or 4 dough rounds at a time for about 1 to 2 minutes, until they are golden brown. Remove, drain and serve piping hot.

Serve with a savory filling such as cheese or cooked meats. Fold over to make a taco. Alternatively, serve with sweet fillings such as sugar, honey, maple syrup or berries, or roll them in cinnamon and sugar.

Trailside tips:

• Pack an "S"-shaped hook: one end fits over a makeshift tripod and the pot is suspended from the other end by its handle. If there's enough wood to light a fire, there is enough to fashion a few basic utensils, such as skewers or a spit.

Pancakes

This is a real favorite, and tastes best when served around the campfire in a skillet or on the griddle. The dry ingredients can be batched together at home.

Makes **12**   Prep. time: **10** mins   Cooking time: **3** mins

3 cups/750 ml	**all-purpose flour**
1 cup/250 ml	**cornmeal**
2 tbsp/30 ml	**baking powder**
3 tbsp/45 ml	**sugar**
1 tsp/5 ml	**salt**
4	**eggs or egg powder equivalent**
1/4 cup/50 ml	**vegetable oil**
3 cups/750 ml	**milk**
2 drops	**vanilla extract**

At camp:

In a large bowl, mix together the flour, cornmeal, baking powder, sugar and salt. Beat the eggs and blend them into the flour mixture, along with the oil, milk and vanilla. Whip with a fork until you have a thin batter.

Allow the batter to rest for a few minutes and it will start to thicken.

Heat a skillet and add 1 tbsp/15 ml oil. Pour in enough batter, about 2 tbsp/30 ml, to make a pancake about 6 in/15 cm in diameter. Cook for 1 to 2 minutes. Flip the pancake and cook for a further minute or so, until golden brown.

Serve with jelly, fruit, honey, lemon juice and sugar.

Honey doughnuts

Camp honey doughnuts are easy and quick to make and delicious to eat when fresh and hot. The key to good doughnuts is the oil temperature — it must be right for the doughnuts to expand and cook properly. If it is too cold, they will turn out too oily; if it is too hot they will burn, so experiment by dropping small pieces of doughnuts in the oil. Once the mixture swells up right away, the temperature is perfect.

Makes **12** doughnuts   Prep. time: **15** mins   Standing time: **3** hours
Cooking time: Seconds!

1 tbsp/15 ml	**active dry yeast**
1/2 cup/125 ml	**warm water**
1	**egg or egg powder equivalent**
1/2 tsp/2 ml	**salt**
3 cups/750 ml	**all-purpose flour**
1 tsp/5 ml	**sugar**
1 tbsp/15 ml	**vegetable oil plus extra for deep-frying**
	honey, to taste
	cinnamon, to taste

At camp:

In a large bowl, mix together the yeast with the warm water. Add the egg, salt, oil, flour and sugar, and mix until you have a firm dough.

Knead the dough on a floured board for 4 or 5 minutes. Leave in a warm place for about 2 hours until the dough has doubled in size.

Roll flat and cut into 1 1/2 in/4 cm squares and leave for a further hour to rise.

When you are ready to deep-fry, pour oil into a large skillet to a depth of 1 1/2 to 2 in/4 to 5 cm, and heat. Drop in balls of dough, two or three at a time. Cook for just seconds and remove the doughnuts when they are golden brown. Drain and serve hot, dipped in honey and sprinkled with cinnamon.

Banana bread

You can make this nutritious banana bread at home — it keeps well on the trail — or you can bake it at the campsite in a Dutch oven. It's wonderful hot from the oven, spread with butter, or tasty as a trail snack.

Makes 1 x 1 lb/450 g loaf   Prep. time: **10** mins
Cooking time: **50–60** mins

3/4 cup/175 ml	honey
1/2 cup/125 ml	butter or oil
2	eggs or egg powder equivalent
4	bananas
1/2 cup/125 ml	buttermilk
1 tsp/5 ml	vanilla extract
2 1/2 cups/625 ml	all-purpose flour
1 tsp/5 ml	baking soda
1 tsp/5 ml	salt
1 cup/250 ml	chopped nuts
1/2 cup/125 ml	chocolate chips

At home:

Preheat the oven to 350°F/180°C. Grease a 9-in/23-cm square pan.
Mix the honey and butter in large bowl, and blend in the eggs. Mash the bananas and add them, with the buttermilk and vanilla, to the mixture. Beat until smooth.
Fold in the flour, baking soda and salt and stir in the nuts and chocolate chips.
Spoon the mixture into the bread pan and bake for 1 hour. Test to see if it is ready by sticking a skewer into the center. If it comes out clean, it is cooked.
Remove from the pan and allow it to cool. Pack in foil — it will keep for several days.

At camp:

Line the base and sides of a Dutch oven with foil.
Follow the directions above to prepare the mixture and spoon it directly onto the foil.
Pile a layer of embers on the lid so that the mixture cooks from top and bottom. Bake for 1 hour. Test as above. Remove from the oven by taking hold of both sides of the foil and lifting the bread out. Allow to cool before serving.

Chocolate muffins

You can bake these muffins at home and freeze until needed or make them in a Dutch oven while out camping. If you make them at home, thaw them the day before you leave and they will keep for about a week under most conditions.

Makes **12**   Prep. time: **10** mins   Cooking time: **15—20** mins

3	**eggs or egg powder equivalent**
1¹/₂ cups/375 ml	**sugar**
²/₃ cup/150 ml	**oil**
¹/₃ cup/75 ml	**pureed applesauce**
1 tbsp/15 ml	**vanilla extract**
1 cup/250 ml	**chopped walnuts**
1 cup/250 ml	**chocolate chips**
2¹/₂ cups/625 ml	**all-purpose flour**
1 tsp/5 ml	**baking powder**
1 tsp/5 ml	**baking soda**
¹/₂ tsp/2 ml	**salt**
1 tbsp/15 ml	**cinnamon, optional**
¹/₂ cup/125 ml	**chocolate milk powder**

At home:
Preheat the oven to 375°F/190°C. With a fork or a whisk, mix together the eggs, sugar, oil, applesauce, vanilla, nuts and chocolate chips. Sift in and blend the flour, baking powder, baking soda, salt, cinnamon and chocolate milk powder.
Spoon the mixture into a 12-cup muffin pan and bake for 15 to 20 minutes or until golden brown.
Pack in airtight bags and freeze until needed.

Or at camp:
Preheat the Dutch oven over the fire embers.
Prepare the mixture as above and spoon into a muffin pan. Bake in the Dutch oven for 20 to 30 minutes or until golden brown.

Weekend gourmet

Camping and feasting — there are few things better than dining out under the stars with fine wine, good food and best friends.

The following recipes will allow you to dine out in style — to enjoy the ambience of eating *al fresco*. The meals are not intended for the lightweight camper although some can certainly be created on a couple of camping stoves. Instead, we have assumed that you are able to transport in all the items you will need to enjoy a gastronomic treat. So load up the tables, rugs, and the grill, and pack candles to add an extra touch of glamour.

Chicken primavera

Primavera literally means "spring style" in Italian and relies on young, fresh and tender vegetables to produce a light, flavorful garnish for the chicken. Follow this with the fruitiness of the Pineapple sundae, opposite, for a memorable dessert.

Serves **8**   Prep. time: **15** mins   Cooking time: **20** mins

4 tbsp/60 ml	**oil**
2 lbs/900 g	**chicken breast, skinned and cut into bite-size cubes**
1/3 cup/75 ml	**cornstarch**
4 cups/1 l	**chicken stock**
1	**head broccoli florets**
1	**green bell pepper, diced**
1	**red bell pepper, diced**
2	**carrots, diced**
2	**onions, finely sliced**
1 lb/450 g	**spaghetti**
2 tbsp/30 ml	**grated Parmesan**
	salt and pepper, to taste

At camp:

In a skillet, heat the oil and sauté the chicken until golden brown and cooked through, about 10 minutes. Remove from the heat and keep warm.

Blend the cornstarch with 1/2 cup/125 ml of the stock to make a smooth paste. Pour the remainder of the stock into a large pan. Set over a medium heat and add the broccoli, peppers, carrot and onion and bring to a boil. Reduce the heat to low and cook until the vegetables are tender, 7 to 10 minutes.

Add the cornstarch paste and stir continuously until the mixture boils and thickens. Add the chicken and heat through.

In a separate pan, bring salted water to a boil and cook the spaghetti on a rolling boil until it is al dente, 8 to 10 minutes. Drain.

Serve the spaghetti in large bowls, topped with the chicken and vegetables. Finish with a sprinkling of grated Parmesan and season to taste.

Pineapple sundae

Serves **8**   Prep. time: **10** mins

2	**fresh pineapples, cut into chunks**
2 cups/500 ml	**sweet orange segments**
2	**bananas, cut into chunks**
4 tbsp/60 ml	**finely chopped crystalized ginger**
4 cups/1 l	**plain yogurt**
2 tsp/10 ml	**vanilla extract**
2 tsp/10 ml	**sugar**

At camp:

Mix the pineapple, orange, banana and most of the ginger together in one bowl.

In a separate bowl, mix the yogurt, vanilla and sugar.

Into glasses or colorful transparent picnic ware, layer alternately the fruit and yogurt mix. Sprinkle the remaining chopped ginger on top to serve.

Floridian lamb kabobs

Delicious lamb kabobs are great for a party. We call this Floridian lamb because, while you will rarely see sheep in the Sunshine State, we do have a lot of orange trees. Make up the marinade the day before, add the lamb and by the time you come to grill it, all the flavors will be absorbed. Follow with Just peachy, a subtle, rum-infused dessert.

Serves **8**   Prep. time: **20** mins   Cooking time: **30** mins

2¹/₂ lbs/1.2 kg	boned lamb, cubed
3 tbsp/45 ml	ground coriander
4 cups/1 l	fresh orange juice
²/₃ cup/150 ml	orange liqueur, optional
1	jalapeno pepper, seeds removed and cut into tiny pieces
6	oranges, peeled, pips removed and cut into slices

At home:

Rub the ground coriander into the cubed meat.

In a large bowl, mix the meat with the orange juice, liqueur and pepper. Cover and marinate in the refrigerator overnight.

Before leaving home, transfer the meat and marinade into a large plastic container. Keep cool.

At camp:

Fire up the grill to a medium heat. Put out two bowls, one for the meat and the other for the orange slices.

Pour the marinade into a small pan, bring to a boil and simmer, uncovered, until it has reduced to a sticky orange sauce. Set aside.

Take a skewer and thread a piece of lamb, then a slice of orange and repeat until the skewer is full. Repeat with the other skewers. Place the skewers on the grill and cook to your liking.

Remove the meat and orange slices from the skewers, arrange on plates and drizzle with the sauce. Serve with Scalloped potatoes (p. 110) and maybe a green salad.

Just peachy

Serves **8** Prep. time: **20** mins

4 lbs/1.8 kg	**fresh peaches, peeled, pitted and sliced**
1¹/₂ tsp/7 ml	**ground ginger**
1¹/₃ cups/325 ml	**heavy cream**
2 tbsp/30 ml	**rum**

At home:

Purée the peaches and ginger and pack into an airtight container. Keep chilled.

At camp:

Empty the peach purée into a large bowl, stir in the heavy cream and rum.
Serve in pretty glasses or bowls.

Goulash

Start with this classic dish that can be prepared quickly if necessary or simmered gently for even richer flavors, leaving you free to mingle with your friends. Follow by serving Fruit grill, opposite, a decadent dessert that can involve everyone in the cooking.

Serves **8**   Prep. time: **10** mins
Cooking time: **20—30** mins (but will simmer happily for longer)

2 tbsp/30 ml	oil
2 lbs/900 g	lean beef, cubed
2	onions, finely chopped
28-oz/800-g	can chopped tomatoes
1	green bell pepper, diced
1	stalk celery, chopped
2 tbsp/30 ml	paprika
1 tsp/5 ml	dried basil
1 tsp/5 ml	marjoram
	salt and pepper, to taste
1 cup/250 ml	sour cream
3 cups/750 ml	medium dried egg noodles
bunch	parsley, chopped

At camp:

Heat the oil in a large pan. Sear the meat in the hot oil until browned on all sides. Remove and set aside.

Sauté the onion for 5 minutes, until softened. Add the tomatoes, bell pepper, celery, paprika, basil, marjoram and season to taste.

Return the meat to the skillet, add the sour cream and stir well to combine all the ingredients. Cover the pan and simmer gently for 30 minutes, stirring occasionally. Approximately 10 minutes before you are ready to serve the goulash, bring a pan of salted water to a boil and plunge the noodles in to cook on a rolling boil for 5 to 8 minutes. Drain thoroughly.

Serve the noodles topped with spoonfuls of rich goulash. Sprinkle chopped parsley over the top for a gourmet finish.

Fruit grill

Serves **8**   Prep. time: **5** mins   Cooking time: **15** mins

16 cups/2.4 kg	**assorted fresh chopped fruits (such as cherries, bananas, apricots, plums, strawberries, pineapple, peaches)**
30	**marshmallows**
1 cup/250 ml	**chocolate chips**
	cream or plain yogurt, to serve

At camp:

Lightly grease a 9 x 13-in/23 x 33-cm baking tray. Spread the chopped fruit evenly over the tray and distribute the marshmallows on top. The aim is to try to cover all the fruit with the marshmallows so that when they melt they form a layer above the fruit.

Sprinkle the chocolate chips on top of the marshmallows.

Cover the tray with foil, making sure all sides are sealed. Then rest the baking tray on the grill for 10 to 15 minutes, to melt the marshmallows and chocolate.

Remove from heat and carefully remove the foil. Allow to cool for about 3 minutes. Slice and serve with cream or plain yogurt.

Vegetarian chili

This chili is not only healthy and wholesome, it is bursting with flavors as well. Follow it with Banana boats, opposite, with a dash of rum to keep out any late evening chill. Although the dessert is best cooked in the embers it can be cooked on a grill or stove. However you cook it, it is delicious.

Serves **6**   Prep. time: **10** mins   Cooking time: **30** mins

1¹/₂ cups/375 ml	vegetable stock
3	zucchini, chopped
14-oz/400-g	can chopped tomatoes
2	carrots, diced
1	green bell pepper, diced
1 tbsp/15 ml	chili powder
1 tsp/5 ml	ground cumin
¹/₂ tsp/2 ml	dried thyme
1¹/₂ cups/375 ml	canned black beans, drained
1¹/₂ cups/375 ml	canned chickpeas, drained
1 tbsp/15 ml	oil
4 cups/1 l	long grain rice
	sour cream, to serve

At camp:

In a large pan, bring the stock to a boil over a medium heat and add the zucchini, tomatoes, carrots, pepper, chili powder, cumin and thyme. Return to a boil, cover and simmer gently for 20 minutes. Do not overcook the vegetables; they should be tender but not mushy.

Add the black beans and chickpeas and increase the temperature to heat through for a further 5 minutes.

In a separate large pan, heat the oil and shoot in the rice, stirring until the grains are coated. Add 8 cups/2 litres of hot water and return to a boil. Stir once and cover. Reduce the heat and simmer for 15 minutes until all the liquid is absorbed.

Serve with some sour cream and a side of Tomato, cucumber and red onion salad (p. 82).

Banana boats

Serves 6   Prep. time: 5 mins   Cooking time: 5 mins

6	**bananas**
1/2 cup/125 ml	**chocolate chips**
1/3 cup/75 ml	**brown sugar**
2 tbsp/30 ml	**rum or cognac**

At camp:

Peel back one flap on each banana so that the whole of one side is exposed. Make sure the flap is still attached at one end. Make a slit lengthwise down the banana, being careful not to cut all the way through. Then gently lever the cut apart to make a cavity.

In this slit, sprinkle chocolate chips, top with brown sugar and drizzle over 1 tbsp/15 ml rum or cognac. Repeat with the other bananas.

Replace the flap of peel and individually wrap the bananas tightly in foil. Place in the embers of the fire for about 5 minutes, or until the chocolate and brown sugar have melted. Pull away the foil and use this as dishes to serve.

Almond chicken

A great summer evening's dinner combination — both this Almond chicken recipe and the Zabaglione, opposite, are packed with flavor, but neither is very heavy so you could even go for a starlight stroll or a midnight swim after the meal.

Serves **4**   Prep. time: **10** mins   Cooking time: **20** mins

1 tbsp/15 ml	**oil**
2	**large chicken breasts, skinned and diced**
1	**onion, finely chopped**
2	**stalks celery, diced**
1	**carrot, thinly sliced**
1/2 cup/125 ml	**almonds, finely chopped**
2 tbsp/30 ml	**lemon juice**
1 cup/250 ml	**light cream**
	salt and pepper, to taste
1/2 cup/125 ml	**croutons or cubes of crusty bread**
1 cup/250 ml	**grated Cheddar cheese**
	rice or noodles, to serve

At camp:

Heat the oil in a large pan over hot embers, add the chicken and sauté for about 10 minutes until golden brown and cooked through. Remove from the pan and set aside to keep warm.

Add the onion, celery, carrot and almonds, and stir to make sure all the ingredients are coated with oil. Sauté gently until the vegetables are tender — 2 to 3 minutes. Return the chicken to the pan, along with the lemon juice and cream. Stir and season to taste. Sprinkle over the croutons and the cheese, and allow to heat through until the cheese melts. Serve on a bed of rice or with noodles.

Zabaglione

Serves **4**   Prep. time: **5** mins   Cooking time: **15–20** mins

5	egg yolks
1/2 cup/125 ml	**sugar**
1/2 cup/125 ml	**Marsala wine**

At camp:

In a large pan, fill water to a depth of 2 in/6 cm and bring to a boil.
In a smaller pan that will sit inside the larger pan, combine the egg yolks and sugar until smooth. Add the Marsala and, stirring continuously, allow the mixture to heat through and thicken. Serve warm as soon as it thickens, in glasses or bowls.

Chicken chasseur

This chicken dish is both delicious and very filling and works well served with fresh crusty bread and a good French country wine. The dessert is a fitting accompaniment as it is light and refreshing after such a hearty main course.

Serves **8**   Prep. time: **10** mins   Cooking time: **20–25** mins

2 tbsp/30 ml	**oil**
8	**chicken breasts, cut into thick strips**
	salt and pepper, to taste
2 tbsp/30 ml	**butter**
2	**onions, finely chopped**
3 cups/750 ml	**sliced mushrooms**
6	**cloves garlic, roughly chopped**
1 tbsp/15 ml	**flour**
1 cup/250 ml	**chicken stock**
1/2 cup/125 ml	**red wine**
4	**large tomatoes, chopped**
pinch	**dried thyme**
	fresh parsley, chopped
	mashed potatoes, to serve

At camp:

Heat the oil in a skillet over a moderate heat and brown the chicken. Turn frequently to ensure thorough cooking and season to taste. Remove the chicken from the pan and keep warm.

Add the butter to the pan and sauté the onion until golden. Add the mushrooms and garlic and sauté for 5 minutes. Stir the flour into the juices until blended and then add the stock, wine, tomatoes and thyme.

Return the chicken to the pan, cover and simmer for about 5 minutes, or until warmed through. Sprinkle over the parsley and season to taste. Serve with creamy mashed potatoes.

Mint chocolate pots

Serves **8**   Prep. time: **10** mins

3/4 cup/175 ml	**sugar**
1/3 cup/75 ml	**unsweetened cocoa**
1/4 cup/50 ml	**all-purpose flour**
21/3 cups/575 ml	**milk**
2	**egg yolks**
11/2 cups/375 ml	**mint chocolate chips**
1 tsp/5 ml	**vanilla extract**
1 tbsp/15 ml	**butter**
2 cups/500 ml	**strawberries, to serve**

At home:

In a large pan, combine the sugar, cocoa and flour and slowly stir in the milk.
Cook over a medium heat, stirring frequently, until the mixture thickens and starts to bubble. Reduce the heat and cook for a further 2 minutes, then remove from heat.
Pour half the mixture into a bowl and beat in the egg yolks. When thoroughly blended, return the contents of the bowl to the pan.
Add the mint chocolate chips and bring back to a gentle bubbling boil, stirring frequently.
Reduce the heat and simmer, stirring occasionally, for a further 2 minutes. Stir in the vanilla and butter and simmer for 1 minute. Pour the mixture into a sealable container, leave to cool, cover and refrigerate.
Transport in the container and keep cool.
Serve with fresh strawberries with their hulls intact, so that they can be dipped into the chocolate.

137

Jambalaya

Jambalaya is a family favorite and we have cooked it many times while camping out in the Ocala National Forest, one of the best places to spot Florida's dwindling population of black bears. Whether you cook it at home or on the trail, it is always memorable. Experiment with the ingredients: add diced chicken breast (skinned) and shrimp to turn it into an even more sumptuous feast. Berries galore, opposite, to follow is a fruity and refreshing dessert.

Serves **8**   Prep. time: **10** mins   Cooking time: **10–15** mins

2 tbsp/30 ml	**oil**
2	**onions, finely chopped**
8	**cloves garlic, crushed**
2 lbs/900 g	**Italian sausages, sliced into chunks**
3 cups/750 ml	**long grain rice**
3 cups/750 ml	**chicken stock**
4	**large tomatoes, chopped**
2	**green bell peppers, sliced**
1 tsp/5 ml	**ground cumin**
1 tbsp/15 ml	**Tabasco**
	salt and pepper, to taste

At camp:

Heat the oil in a large skillet or wok over a moderate heat. Sauté the onions and garlic for about 2 minutes, until they are softened. Add the sausage and cook for a further minute. Stir in the rice, stock, tomatoes, bell pepper, cumin, Tabasco and seasoning. Combine well and bring to a boil. Cover and simmer for 10 to 15 minutes, stirring occasionally, until the rice is soft.

Remove from the heat and let stand, covered, until all the liquid has been absorbed. Fluff up with a fork before serving.

Berries galore

Serves **8**   Prep. time: **5** mins   Cooking time: **10–15** mins

2 cups/500 ml	**wild or brown rice**
4 cups/1,000 ml	**fresh berries (such as blackberries, blueberries, huckleberries, raspberries)**
2 cups/500 ml	**water**
1¹/₂ cups/375 ml	**sugar**
¹/₂ tsp/2 ml	**salt**
1 tbsp/15 ml	**cornstarch**
2 tbsp/30 ml	**lemon juice**
	light cream or yogurt, to serve

At camp:

Cook the rice in boiling water until soft. Remove from heat and keep warm.

Put the whole berries, 1¹/₂ cups/375 ml water, the sugar and the salt into a pan and stir over a gentle heat until the sugar is completely dissolved.

Blend the cornstarch with ¹/₂ cup/125 ml water to make a thin paste, and stir it into the fruit syrup. Warm over a medium heat until the sauce thickens and clears. Add the lemon juice and rice and heat through.

Remove from heat and serve slightly warm in bowls, with yogurt or light cream.

Stuffed trout

If you are a successful angler you may be able to catch enough fish for this meal. If not, buy them. The basil and rosemary impart a wonderful flavor to the fish which should just fall off the bone when cooked over the fire. Follow very simply with fresh fruit and chocolate — everyone's desire.

Serves **8**   Prep. time: **15** mins   Cooking time: **15** mins

8	**medium-size trout**
8	**cloves garlic, crushed**
4	**lemons, 3 halved and 1 cut into 8 slices**
8	**sprigs fresh basil**
8	**sprigs fresh rosemary**
	salt and pepper, to taste

At camp:

Fire up the grill to a medium-high heat.

Prepare the trout by cleaning and removing heads.

Stuff the inside cavity with 1 slice of lemon, 1 crushed garlic clove and a sprig each of basil and rosemary. Season with salt and pepper. Wrap each fish in foil and cook over direct heat for 15 to 18 minutes. Alternatively, fry the fish up in a large skillet. It is cooked when it flakes easily.

Remove the sprigs before serving, and apportion pieces of lemon to each plate to squeeze over the fish.

Trailside tips:

• Save some lemon to rub on your hands after cooking and eating. The juice will remove any fishy smells.

• Don't be afraid to spice up your food, especially on a cold night, with plenty of garlic as well as paprika or cayenne pepper.

Chocolate fondue

Serves **8**   Prep. time: **5** mins   Cooking time: **10** mins

3 cups/750 ml	**milk chocolate chips**
1 cup/250 ml	**milk**
4 cups/1,000 ml	**fresh fruit (such as apples, bananas, pears, strawberries), cut into large chunks**

At camp:

Melt the chocolate chips in a pan over a very low heat. Be careful it doesn't burn.
Add the milk and stir continuously until the mixture starts to bubble gently.
Remove from the heat and serve immediately in the pot, placed in the center of the
group. Everyone dips chunks of fruit into the chocolate and if a piece of fruit is lost into
the chocolate a forfeit has to be performed by the offender!

Resources & Acknowledgments

FURTHER READING

Adkinson, R., *Hiking Grand Canyon National Park*, Falcon, 1997

Brill, S., *Identifying and Harvesting Edible and Medicinal Plants*, Quill, 1994

Couplan, F., *The Encyclopedia of Edible Plants of North America*, Keats Publishing, 1998

Davenport, G., *Wilderness Survival*, Stackpole Books, 1998

Frommer's National Parks of the American West, *Hungry Minds*, 1998

Molvar, E., *Hiking Zion and Bryce Canyon National Parks*, Falcon, 1997

National Geographic Guide to the National Parks of North America, National Geographic, 2003

Schneider, B., *Exploring Canyonlands and Arches National Parks*, Falcon, 1997

Schneider, B,. *Hiking Yellowstone National Park*, Falcon, 2003

Stilwell, A., *The Encyclopedia of Survival Techniques*, The Lyons Press, 2000

The National Audubon Society Field Guides offer the most comprehensive description of the flora and fauna of North America. Worth reading are:

National Audubon Society *Field Guide to Birds*

National Audubon Society *Field Guide to Mushrooms*

National Audubon Society *Field Guide to North American Trees* (Western & Eastern editions)

National Audubon Society *Field Guide to North American Wildflowers*

National Audubon Society *Field Guide to Weather*

CAMPING SUPPLIERS

The following are websites for suppliers of camping and outdoors equipment. Some, like Coleman, are manufacturers with distributors in both the northern and southern hemispheres. Use these websites to find out what is available and what best suits your needs. Always remember when buying outdoor clothing and equipment, it pays to buy the best — don't skimp — because your life could depend on it.

www.berghaus.com Outdoor clothing, knapsacks, footwear

www.coleman.com Everything you need for the camp kitchen and campsite

www.lowealpine.com Outdoor clothing, knapsacks, boots

www.optimus.se Stoves

www.trangia.se Stoves

PICTURE CREDITS

The publisher would like to thank the following photographers for their contributions:

Andrew Cox pages 13, 74, 133 Chris Fryer pages 114–5 Getty Images pages 38, 141 Mats Hogberg pages 2, 8, 16, 21, 23, 28, 32, 34, 37, 47, 50, 57, 63, 64, 69, 73, 76, 79–80, 83, 87, 88, 92, 96, 99, 104, 107, 111, 114, 117, 124, 129, 131, 139 Amanda Leung pages 67, 91, 125, 127   NIAC pages 4, 27, 41, 135 Photonica page 31 Gill Nisbet pages 11, 50–1, 64–5, 76–7 Tracy Timson pages 1, 24, 113 *Trail* magazine pages 15, 18, 54, 92–3

Index